Leveraging the ePortfolio
for Integrative Learning

Leveraging the ePortfolio for Integrative Learning

A Faculty Guide to Classroom Practices for Transforming Student Learning

Candyce Reynolds and Judith Patton

Foreword by
Terry Rhodes

STERLING, VIRGINIA

Published by Stylus Publishing, LLC
22883 Quicksilver Drive
Sterling, Virginia 20166-2102

Library of Congress Cataloging-in-Publication Data
Reynolds, Candyce.
Leveraging the ePortfolio for integrative learning : a faculty guide
to classroom practices for transforming student learning / Candyce
Reynolds and Judith Patton. – First edition.
   pages cm
Includes bibliographical references and index.
ISBN 978-1-57922-899-6 (cloth : alk. paper)
ISBN 978-1-57922-900-9 (pbk. : alk. paper)
ISBN 978-1-57922-901-6 (library networkable eedition)
ISBN 978-1-57922-902-3 (consumer e-edition)
1. Electronic portfolios in education.
2. Transformative learning. I. Patton, Judith. II. Title.
LB1029.P67R46 2014
371.39–dc23
                                                        2013048768
13-digit ISBN: 978-1-57922-899-6 (cloth)
13-digit ISBN: 978-1-57922-900-9 (paperback)
13-digit ISBN: 978-1-57922-901-6 (library networkable e-edition)
13-digit ISBN: 978-1-57922-902-3 (consumer e-edition)

Printed in the United States of America

All first editions printed on acid-free paper
that meets the American National Standards Institute
Z39-48 Standard.

Bulk Purchases

Quantity discounts are available for use in
workshops and for staff development.
Call 1-800-232-0223

First Edition, 2014

10   9   8   7   6   5   4   3   2   1

To our past and future students

Contents

viii   Contents

Foreword

Portfolios of student work are not new; digital portfolios (ePortfolios) have been around since the late 1990s. EDUCAUSE tells us that ePortfolios are now in use in over half of American colleges and universities. Evidence is emerging that when done well, engaging students with ePortfolios as part of their education is a high-impact/highly effective practice correlated with both improved retention and graduation, as well as deeper student learning on a range of learning outcomes beyond the few that standardized tests address. Hart Research Associates' surveys tell us that employers increasingly express interest in seeing what students can do through the actual projects, papers, presentations, performances, and so on that they have completed as part of their education, not simply a traditional transcript or resume; indeed, they want to see an ePortfolio of students' actual work and reflection on their learning and capabilities.

At the same time, policymakers and politicians have been calling for greater access to and completion of college educations for a stronger global economy (and occasionally for a strengthened democracy and civic life). Often these calls focus primarily on numbers of graduates or completers with little attention to either the range and type of learning or the quality of the learning that accompanies the completion. Much attention has been focused on the use of technology and digital innovations to increase access and completion with heavy emphasis on large-scale provision of content, courses, and training.

As a result, many faculty, administrators, and students have been encouraged to explore digital options and opportunities—many of which address one or another of the demands for change and transformation in higher education, but few seem to encompass the multi-faceted, developmental, and idiosyncratic process that is deep, integrative, quality learning.

This volume is a welcome response to that need, linking together the theoretical, conceptual, and practical dimensions of one of the most ubiquitous and promising extant technologies that integrates what we know about what works for enhanced student learning and success.

I have known the authors, Candyce Reynolds and Judy Patton, for many years, having had the privilege of participating in University Studies at Portland State University for six years before coming to the Association of American Colleges and Universities. Their experience maps the path of so many who have engaged and are engaging with ePortfolios as they explore ways to respond to the multitude of calls for transforming higher education.

The authors do five things that are essential for helping anyone to think about using or expanding ePortfolio initiatives in their own classes, programs, or institutions. They

1. make the critical first argument that ePortfolios are not a technology, but rather a framework for learning;
2. keep the focus on student learning;
3. provide a rich research base for the advantages of an ePortfolio approach for faculty, educational professionals, and students;
4. recognize the absolute necessity of high-level integrative learning as essential to student success in this century; and
5. provide a set of examples and prompts that are practical and doable for novice and advanced ePortfolio users that will assist in making better choices for adopting and adapting ePortfolios as an integral approach to learning and teaching.

If these five dimensions of ePortfolio practice are attended to, ePortfolio engagement holds great promise for fundamentally enhancing student learning and success.

Anyone who has or has been around infants and small children knows that children have an amazing capacity from birth onward for soaking up information and integrating it in order to develop and perform complex tasks without any formal education, for instance, walking, talking, playing, drawing, and experimenting. Child development is truly stunning and underappreciated and undervalued by most of us; we take it for granted until we see it *not* happening. Currently, our educational systems treat most of formal education as a collection of discrete endeavors requiring attention only at specified times and in particular locations. Even in higher education, the efforts to integrate the learning process typically involve passing references to other courses, experiences, and perhaps readings from other disciplines; or team-teaching or guest appearances that bring new and different insights into the main topic at hand. Integration of the learning is left primarily to the student. After all, that is how we know who our best students are; they will "get it" and be able to accomplish a level of integration of knowledge.

ePortfolios are not the panacea. ePortfolios are a framework that allows all of us working in higher education (including our students) to have a shared space to inquire; to explore; to challenge; to achieve; to discover; and, yes, to assess how we're doing. The authors take these lofty ideas and goals and help us translate them into practical steps that we, as educational professionals, can take to achieve them. For example, the authors cover the importance of having articulated learning outcomes at course and program levels in order to create assignments that actually elicit the learning encompassed in the outcomes; how to think about and pose questions around technology to use; how assessment can be a very useful learning tool; and how departments, as well as general education, can connect with each other and use ePortfolios with their students to achieve common purposes and outcomes.

The authors use direct language to lead novice and experienced colleagues through the pieces and the whole that are ePortfolio. Overarching the authors' approach is the point that ePortfolios are the best opportunity we have at an affordable cost to help our students and educational professionals to reconstruct the abilities to integrate learning through processes that facilitate meaning making at complex and sophisticated levels required for college and life success. ePortfolios are a means to take college and university teaching and learning from a reductionist, fractured set of events toward a more coherent, intentional, and meaningful whole; that is, from *my work* to *our work*, in partnership with professional colleagues, students, community members, and others.

—Terry Rhodes
Vice President for the Office of Quality, Curriculum and Assessment,
Association of American Colleges and Universities

Preface

This book has been a long time coming. We have been using ePortfolios for over 15 years, beginning in Portland State University's general education program, University Studies, and in our disciplinary programs and courses. In an effort to enhance and assess student learning on the four goals of general education, faculty teaching in the program took on the challenge of using web-based portfolios in the yearlong first-year courses. Little did we know that we would learn so much about student learning in the process of rolling out and developing these portfolios. We learned not only that ePortfolios are a way to help faculty assess courses and programs but also that if we supported the development of the ePortfolio with pedagogical practices, students integrated and demonstrated their learning far beyond our expectations. We found the use of ePortfolios can be not only truly transformational for our students in helping them develop their identities and understanding, but also transformative for faculty in helping them understand and appreciate the complexity of students' learning. We are ePortfolio converts.

Interest in ePortfolios has exploded in the past 15 years or so. Faculty and administrators have begun to see that an ePortfolio provides opportunities for deeper learning and easier and more comprehensive ways to assess student learning than a traditional paper portfolio. In addition, part of the excitement over ePortfolios has to do with their potential to help students integrate their learning. Integrative learning has been identified as an important outcome of higher education. The Association of American Colleges and Universities (AAC&U) (2007a) named it as one of four essential outcomes for undergraduate education. While the ability to connect and apply knowledge has always been important, AAC&U's prioritizing integrative learning gives notice to institutions of higher education that this kind of learning, while it may come naturally, needs to be fostered and nurtured in college students to meet the needs of the 21st century, and ePortfolios are frequently touted as the vehicle to get there. All too often, however, when leaders of institutions jump on the ePortfolio bandwagon, they assume that students can and should be able to make sense of their learning. They believe that if students have access to an ePortfolio tool, the learning part will just come naturally. It is no surprise that faculty and administrators are often disappointed by some of the lackluster ePortfolios students submit.

Students can produce brilliant ePortfolios on their own. Some students get it; many do not. Our experience is that all students have the potential to create substantive ePortfolios if supported by pedagogical practices that facilitate integrative learning. This book, then, focuses on the use of the ePortfolio as a *pedagogy* that facilitates integrative learning. We argue for the importance of engaging students in integrative learning practices embedded in the classroom and provide faculty and staff with easy-to-use and practical strategies for building an integrative ePortfolio into their curriculum or program.

This book focuses on helping faculty and administrators facilitate students' developing truly integrative student learning ePortfolios. Part One of the book describes the key concepts: the ePortfolio and integrative learning, and how to include integrative learning and ePortfolios in your classroom or program. Chapter 1 describes an ePortfolio, explains what makes a good portfolio, and explores underlying learning theory that supports the practice. Chapter 2 focuses on defining *integrative learning*, discussing its importance in higher education, and explores ways those in higher education have begun to assess it. Chapter 3 describes how to make integrative learning a goal in courses or programs.

Students cannot create integrative learning ePortfolios without appropriate scaffolding, the building blocks that need to be in the classroom. Part Two offers several chapters on classroom practices and assignments that support the development of integrative learning. Chapter 4 highlights developing reflective practice skills in students. What makes a good reflection prompt? Can you make someone reflect? Chapter 5 focuses on activities that help students make connections in a multitude of ways, between course content and their personal lives, course-course connections, course-major connections, and bridging theory to practice. Chapter 6 targets activities that promote the development of self-directed learning. Chapter 7 focuses on activities that address the role of communication in the ePortfolio. How does one present an integrative ePortfolio? What does it look like? Who is the audience? What does the design say to the reader? What is the most appropriate way to communicate?

While the pedagogical practices that support the creation of an integrative learning ePortfolio are the focus of this book, we can't ignore the importance of the *e* part of the ePortfolio. Part Three addresses practical aspects of helping students create their ePortfolios. Chapter 8 describes aspects faculty should consider when assigning an ePortfolio, including activities for creating ePortfolio structures and issues of privacy and control. Chapter 9 offers instructions for using free web-based software.

Part Four of this book rounds out our discussion of ePortfolios. As ePortfolios are a way of documenting learning, this book would not be complete without a discussion of how ePortfolios can be assessed. While this is not the primary focus of the book, Chapter 10 specifically explores ways that rubrics can be used to evaluate ePortfolios. Consistent with the nature of this book, it offers practical suggestions of how to use rubrics in a course or program. In Chapter 11, we offer some parting thoughts.

INTENDED AUDIENCES AND WAYS OF USING THIS BOOK

This book is first and foremost a practical guide for faculty and staff who want to help their students integrate their learning. Our experience has shown us that the magic derived from ePortfolios happens when the classroom practices support ePortfolio development. This book is for beginning and advanced users of ePortfolios, and those who are just starting or considering the use of ePortfolios should find Part One to be especially helpful in conceptualizing the addition of ePortfolios to their pedagogy. Even those who are active ePortfolio users should find Part Two particularly useful for improving pedagogy.

Our hope is that a faculty or staff member in a high school, college, or university can pick up this book, skim a few chapters, then go to class the next day and use some of the ideas presented here. Many of the activities can be used straight from the book without much adaptation to a particular course. While this book is clearly intended to be used by faculty who are or are considering using ePortfolios, many will find that the concepts and activities presented here are useful for integrative learning even without an ePortfolio.

In addition, those who work with faculty on teaching, staff at faculty development centers, and instructional technologists will find these concepts helpful as they assist faculty to include ePortfolios or to think about integrative learning in their classes. Student affairs professionals will also find many of the activities appropriate when working with students in various capacities. As integrative learning in higher education involves learning that happens outside the classroom, student affairs professionals are key in helping students make connections between curricular and cocurricular activities.

Administrators of programs or institutions will also find this book useful by providing a framework for understanding the role ePortfolios can play in improving student learning and by providing ideas about how to help their staff move an ePortfolio initiative forward. Chapter 8 offers a perspective on larger issues, such as developing an ePortfolio structure, privacy, and control. This chapter is particularly helpful to administrators as they consider embarking on implementing an ePortfolio.

Faculty and administrators should find Part Two and Chapter 10 particularly helpful as they plan course, program, or institutional assessment.

WHAT THIS BOOK DOES NOT DO

While this book provides an overview of the concept of integrative learning and describes the basics of what defines an ePortfolio, this is not *the* definitive book on ePortfolios or integrative learning; it is user oriented. In addition, this book is intentionally short and practical and does not include a plethora of ideas and activities for engaging students in the creation of integrative learning ePortfolios. Our aim is to include examples of activities you can use that will spark your imagination. Since faculty are endlessly creative, they can use the examples here as a springboard to inventing their own activities and assignments.

Acknowledgments

This book would not have been possible without the students and colleagues we have worked with over the years, especially in the University Studies general education program at Portland State University and the growing ePortfolio community internationally. At Portland State University, our students have taught us directly the value of ePortfolios and what works and what doesn't. Several student mentors in the University Studies program have contributed greatly to our understanding of the impact of ePortfolios and how the process actually works for students, especially Sarah Svati Iannarone, Tyler Vaslev, Beth LaPensee, Christopher Ross, Wende Garrison, and Melissa Pirie, as well as many others. Their honest feedback and support of our trials and errors is greatly appreciated. Our colleague Yves Labissiere has been in the ePortfolio business alongside us right from the beginning. His teaching practices and his thoughtful and insightful observations have informed our own practices in the classroom and our thinking and will continue to do so. Michael Flower, a big thinker and gracious, thoughtful colleague in University Studies, has also contributed to our thinking.

Wende Garrison started as a student mentor in University Studies and fell in love with ePortfolios and has since become an expert in the field, helping us in so many ways. She has been a stalwart supporter of our work, challenging us to think and develop our ideas as well as calling on those of us who are ePortfolio enthusiasts to walk our talk. She established a professional network, Out of Practice, to support those of us who teach ePortfolios in making and maintaining our own ePortfolios, which has been invaluable in helping us understand them better. The ePortfolio community is small (but growing) and mighty, anchored by the able leadership of Trent Batson and Judy Batson through the international ePortfolio professional organization the Association for Authentic, Experiential and Evidence-Based

AAEEBL

Learning. We are thankful for support and feedback from many colleagues over the years, including Helen Chen, Tracy Penny-Light, Barbara Cambridge, Darren Cambridge, Kathleen Yancey, Gail Ring, Shane Sutherland, and Nancy McCoy-Wozniak. We have been especially blessed to have been able to work closely with Melissa Peet, through her ePortfolio project funded by the Fund for the Improvement of Postsecondary Education. She has taught us much about the scaffolding necessary to engage students in the development of a meaningful portfolio. We are thankful too for the insights and great teaching ideas from those we have met through the project: Jeffrey Yan, Caryn Chaden, Jessica Bacal, Myra Sabir, A. T. Miller, Barbara Ramirez, and Stacey Fenton.

We have benefited from a core group of colleagues (we call ourselves the League of Busy Brains) at Portland State University who have met regularly to support each other in our professional writing. Thank you, Dannelle Stevens, Ellen West, and Micki Caskey. Special thanks to Dannelle, who is an inspirational teacher of writing practice and an incredible cheerleader. We wouldn't have been able to do this without her help.

Of course, we need to acknowledge our families and friends. Candyce thanks her partner, John Moore, who never asked, When is this thing going to be done?; and her son, Berkeley Moore, who was patient when she couldn't attend to him during writing frenzies and taught him so much about procrastination. Learn from her words, not her actions. Also Candyce thanks her dear friends Birgitta von Schlumperger, Laurel Singer, Rita Smith, Denise Peloquin, Phyllis Richardson, Betsy Reese, Mary Sepulveda, and Eve Durand, who always asked about our progress and always had faith that we would finish. Judy thanks her family, too—Bob, her husband and best friend, who always asked when it would be done. She is particularly grateful to her daughter, Kris, for all the long talks about teaching, learning, ePortfolios, and assessment; her son, Zach, for being impressed that his mom even tried to write a book; and, finally, to her grandchildren, Caitrian and Dash, who gave lots of hugs for encouragement. She also is very appreciative of the words of support from her sister, Carol Blackerby, and her sister-in-law, Wendy Ullman, and of her colleagues Karin Magaldi and Devon Allen, who quietly gave her the confidence to finish the book, and that it would be a good thing.

We would like to thank those who allowed us to reprint their example ePortfolios: Natalie Lyons, Portland State University; Heather McCambly, Portland State University; Sarah Kutten, Portland State University; Evan Goodwin, Clemson University and University of Oregon; Mary Katherine Watson, Georgia Institute of Technology; Wende Garrison, Portland State University; Slade Sapora, Tillamook High School; and Kelly Breitbuecher, Portland State University.

Thank you to those who allowed us to reprint their useful assignment instructions and rubrics: Yves Labissiere, Portland State University; Jeanne Enders, Portland State University; Michael Flowers, Portland State University; Barbara Walvoord, University of Notre Dame; Steven Jones, Georgia College and State University;

Joan Vandervelde, University of Wisconsin, Stout; and Terry Rhodes, Association of American Colleges and Universities.

Finally, we would like to thank our publisher, John von Knorring, who worked with us through several iterations of our book proposal and was endlessly patient with our questions and our slow progress to the finish line. We thank him for the opportunity to share what we have learned through the years.

Introduction

ePortfolios are popping up everywhere—at high schools, colleges, and universities—as administrators and educators discover the rich opportunities they provide for promoting and assessing student learning (e.g., Chen, Penny Light, & Ittleson, 2012; Stefani, Mason, & Pegler, 2007). Even governmental entities (e.g., the state of Minnesota) are sponsoring ePortfolio platforms for their citizens (see www .efoliominnesota.com). Through ePortfolios, students have the opportunity to discover and explore their role as a learner, make connections, and more intentionally integrate their learning. ePortfolios are also a plus for administrators and faculty as they provide a more authentic way of evaluating student and program success.

However, as Internet access, web authoring tools, and ePortfolio software have become more available and accessible, it has been almost too easy for people to create ePortfolios. Although ePortfolios can provide wonderful opportunities for students to learn and for program coordinators to use for assessment, they can end up being glorified electronic file cabinets with little substance or meaning, especially if the attention is on providing the technology or on creating easy-to-assess ePortfolios. Students do some assigned activities, write short reflections, and maybe add a picture or two, and voilà, they have an ePortfolio, merely another assignment. Sadly, these ePortfolios are often disappointments to students, faculty, and administrators. We argue that ePortfolios can meet the goal of advancing and documenting student learning well *if* we provide the necessary classroom supports to make this happen.

We began using ePortfolios in 1998 when they were just beginning to be used in higher education. ePortfolios seem to be a perfect fit for our yearlong, first-year course in the new and innovative general education program, University Studies, at Portland State University (PSU). Since 1994 we had been using paper portfolios to assess student learning on four goals: communication, ethics and social responsibility, the diversity of human experience, and inquiry and critical thinking. We believed

1

and found that portfolios were a great way for students to make connections about what they were learning in their first-year courses as well as outside of them. These portfolios also provided the program with great material to use for assessing learning outcomes. ePortfolios seemed to be a way to enhance technology learning (part of the communication goal), save our students and faculty the burden of carrying huge binders, and ease portfolio assessment.

We provide examples from the University Studies program throughout the book, so we include here some background on the program for context for those examples. University Studies is a four-level general education program. All of a student's required general education takes place in this program, through the first to final year of a student's undergraduate education. ePortfolios are used in the first year-long course, Freshman Inquiry, taken by all students. To date, a significant number of students enrolled in the second-year course, Sophomore Inquiry, are also using ePortfolios.

Through our work as faculty and administrators in this program, we learned that helping students create deep and meaningful ePortfolios means managing the tension among the technology of the ePortfolio tool, program assessment opportunities, and promoting deep learning, a hard balancing act. Students and faculty are often enamored with the bells and whistles technology can provide. In addition, programs and faculty are increasingly being asked to be accountable, and assessment can easily take over in the classroom. However, we have learned that intentionally making learning the center of ePortfolio creation can be transformational for the student and for the faculty, and it actually helps create authentic assessment for courses and programs.

Parallel to the development of our ePortfolios, the academic community was beginning to focus on the need for integrative learning in our college students, and using ePortfolios seemed a natural fit. In 2004 leaders from the Carnegie Foundation for the Advancement of Teaching and the Association of American Colleges and Universities (AAC&U) came together with leaders (including Judy Patton) from 10 campuses to explore integrative learning and how campuses were helping students pursue their education in more intentionally connected ways and to create opportunities for integrating learning rather than expecting it to happen on its own. This work came from an understanding that, at least from high school on, students are taught that knowledge comes in pretty little packages called a *subject* or a *course*. We teach students to learn the facts, ideas, and skills associated with our courses and then test them. As Huber and Hutchings (2004) note, "The very structures of academic life encourage students to see their courses as isolated requirements to complete" (p. 1). In our increasingly complex world, however, this project and the broader academic community called for our students to be able to connect the knowledge they are learning and apply it to solving the problems of the day.

This new emphasis on integrative learning gave us a language to think about our work with a sharper focus. As we continued to work on improving our ePortfolio practice, we focused on developing and experimenting with classroom activities and assignments that intentionally help students make connections between all parts of their lives. And we have become students of others who are doing the same thing, learning from their successful experiences of building integrative learning ePortfolios.

This book is about helping students integrate their learning through the use of ePortfolios, which can look really cool and are fun to make and provide artifacts for assessment. We are primarily interested, however, in providing you with tools to help your students build an ePortfolio that has and makes meaning.

Figure I.1 illustrates our framework for practice. This book discusses four areas of classroom practices and activities that provide the bedrock (or the base of this pyramid) for integrative learning (the center of the pyramid). The outcome of this learning is documented in the ePortfolio (the pinnacle of the pyramid). The figure also illustrates the roles technology and assessment play in an institution's use of an ePortfolio. Considering issues related to technology and teaching students how to use technology aids in the creation of an ePortfolio. And through the ePortfolio, faculty, programs, and institutions have the ability to assess students' integrative learning, and more.

We have written this book in answer to the many people who have attended our presentations at conferences or have visited our campus and wondered how we got our students to create ePortfolios that exhibit the depth of learning they see in our students. It is not an easy road. As shown in the chapters that follow, the true work of creating a transformational ePortfolio is not in the actual making of the ePortfolio— web design, filling out reflection prompts, choosing pictures—but in the process of integrating one's learning. The magic can happen through classroom activities and assignments.

Figure I.1
Integrative Learning ePortfolio Framework

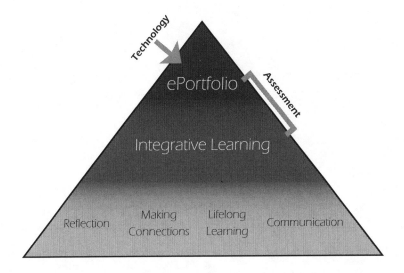

Key Concepts

Part One introduces the key concepts of the book—ePortfolios and integrative learning—and addresses the top part of the framework in Figure Part 1.1. The chapters in this section seek to answer the following questions.

Chapter 1: What is an ePortfolio? How can it be used? What is an integrative ePortfolio? What do ePortfolios look like?

Chapter 2: What is integrative learning? Why is it important, especially in higher education? Can we teach it? How can an ePortfolio contribute to integrative learning?

Chapter 3: How do you integrate integrative learning into a course or program? How do you develop integrative learning outcomes for your course? How can you use an ePortfolio in your course or program? What is the integrative learning ePortfolio process? What does the process look like in an actual course?

Figure Part 1.1
Integrative ePortfolio Guiding Framework

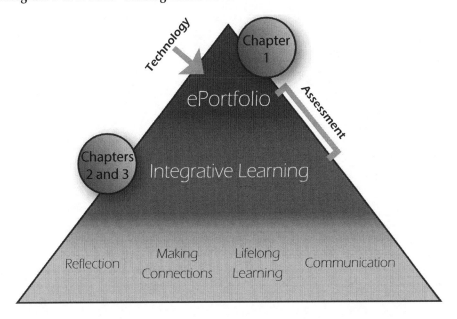

ePortfolios as a Tool for Integrative Learning

Judy's story: I started using portfolios in Freshman Inquiry, a yearlong first-year course in 1995. This interdisciplinary themed course, Embracing Einstein's Universe: Language, Culture, and Relativity, was part of the general education program. While I thought the portfolio was a good idea, I became a real convert at the end of the first year. The students over and over again talked about how important the end-of-the-year portfolio was to their understanding of that whole year's experience. In the final reflection section of the Freshman Inquiry ePortfolio, one student put it like this:

To say this course has been eye-opening would be a gross understatement. I can honestly say that I have come a long way in my thinking about the way I live my life, even how I form my own identity. I have realized that I personally have a responsibility to myself, my community and to the planet to ensure the actions I take are responsible and ethical. Our society faces big problems to which there is no single solution. It is my hope that as I come to understand myself and my world more throughout the course of my academic career, I may be a part of the solution and not the problem. Either we will achieve the miraculous and solve all our problems, or we will ultimately destroy ourselves. I remain an optimist.

Another wrote,

The readings from class about how we develop our personal identities in relation to what we learn about our world and ourselves through the people around us gave me a new and more forgiving lens through which to view my behavior and experiences, and it helped me understand where my own attitudes came from. It also showed me that while true, I am very much a product of my environment, I have a hand in creating the environment and therefore also in creating the identity and experiences of others—that is a huge responsibility.

I could see that collecting all the students' work in the ePortfolios, asking students to make connections between the various activities and assignments in class with their lives, and ending the course with a completed ePortfolio made their learning real and significant. We had been working on the portfolio all year, but the process of putting together that final portfolio brought all the experiences—the readings, discussions, assignments, community-based learning work—together. Those final reflections about their learning over the year were stunning. One student said, "Creating the ePortfolio was the single most important assignment I have ever done in all of my education. I can see and talk about what I have learned and see how all the experiences come together to make a greater whole." The students talked about the ways the various experiences connected, not only one assignment to another but to their lives and to a growing understanding of who they were as learners and as people in the world. They understood that they needed to know more and that they had big decisions to make in their lives they were not yet able to make. These types of experiences were the beginning of our journey to ePortfolios.

Just open your e-mail, or jump into any chat about learning and technology or careers and you will see conversations about ePortfolios, which are becoming a promising practice for helping students and others learn.

According to Lorenzo and Ittleson (2005),

> E-Portfolios are a valuable learning and assessment tool. An e-portfolio is a digitized collection of artifacts, including demonstrations, resources, and accomplishments that represent an individual, group, or institution. This collection can be comprised of text-based, graphic, or multimedia elements archived on a CD-Rom or DVD. . . . E-portfolios encourage reflection. (p. 2)

The following are what Garrison (Garrison & Ring, 2013) identifies as components of what she calls a "true ePortfolio":

- It is digital (meaning it can be found online).
- It contains evidence of the author's experiences and accomplishments.
- It contains reflection.

The uses for an ePortfolio are varied, for example, advising, career planning, undergraduate learning and assessment, faculty promotion and tenure, and institutional. An ePortfolio provides a digital representation of one's work. The focus of this book is on helping you understand and facilitate the creation of student integrative learning ePortfolios that are designed to advance student learning and, at the same time, can be used for student and program assessment. In this chapter, we explore a bit of the history of ePortfolios, including their roots in paper-based portfolios; define what ePortfolios are and how they have been used in the academy; introduce the concept of integrative learning ePortfolios; and then present a variety of examples to help you visualize using ePortfolios in your own classroom. Finally, we explore ways learning theory helps us understand the success of ePortfolios and how they can inform the practices discussed throughout the book.

FROM HARD-COPY PORTFOLIOS TO EPORTFOLIOS

Student portfolios are nothing new and in fact have been used in a variety of disciplines to help students make meaning and to assess their work. These hard-copy portfolios typically contain a collection of artifacts that represent a student's work. Students are asked to collect their best work and to sometimes reflect on this work. The fields of writing, visual arts, architecture, and graphic design have long used the portfolio, assembled in file folders or notebooks, to function as a sample and a showcase of a student's work. Students of writing often include required essays about the work they created and the progress they see or do not see in their writing. Student portfolios in these and other fields have proven to be an excellent way to help students demonstrate their proficiency to their professors and to outside entities and can even support their entry into the job market. A sample of one's work as a graphic designer, for example, is a much more concrete representation of ability than a line on a résumé.

In the mid-1990s several universities began a change process that furthered portfolio development on campuses beyond the writing and arts fields. Seeking to address criticisms from external constituents, as well as from inside academia, institutional leaders realized they needed to demonstrate the real value of the education they were offering to their students. Portfolios became a central way to demonstrate student learning and foster the expansion of a learner-centered environment. The movement included more active teaching strategies to increase and deepen learning and more assessment of learning to address the accountability challenge. At the time, portfolios seemed an effective way to satisfy many goals of the new programs.

In response to increasing accountability pressures and the move to a more student-centered program, students began to demonstrate their learning through hard-copy portfolios before making the transition to ePortfolios. Such was the case at PSU's University Studies program and also at Alverno College. In programs that went from hard copy to digital, those who experienced the transition learned important lessons. As students began using digital media, the experience of creating and using the portfolio changed.

In our program's move to ePortfolios, we found that ePortfolios facilitated the connection between our students' course work and the world and broke down students' misconception that a final exam means the content and experience of a course is done, and that one course is just that, a course, completed.

Through the process of creating an ePortfolio, we found that students developed a variety of learning habits and skills we did not see when they were creating hard-copy portfolios. Labissiere and Reynolds (2004) outline the added benefits:

> An eportfolio requires the development of several skill sets, each of which enhances the student's ability to engage more deeply with what has already been learned. For example, hyperlinking, which is the primary activity of building a website, forces students to make new connections with what has previously been learned. Such hyperlinking practices, we argue, encourage metacognitive skills development. (pp. 2–3)

Table 1.1
Differences in Hard-Copy Versus ePortfolios

Hard-Copy Portfolio	ePortfolio
Work done by an individual	Work done by individual but can be a collaborative effort
Limited audience—generally instructor/artificial	Students control who can see but can be used in multiple ways for multiple audiences
Difficult to keep and store over time	Online storage
	Hyperlinking—critical thinking exercise in and of itself
Viewed usually from beginning to end, one page at a time	Reader creates own journey using links and navigation system
	Emphasis on what students can do
May include student reflection on work, rarely over more than one course	Creates opportunity for student reflection and integrating learning
Primarily written work	Students can demonstrate learning in multiple modes—visual, oral, written, video

Note. Adapted from "Using Electronic Portfolios as a Pedagogical Practice to Enhance Student Learning," by Y. Labissiere & C. Reynolds, 2004, *Inventio, 2*(6). Copyright 2004 by Y. Labissierre & C. Reynolds.

In addition, Labissiere and Reynolds (2004) cite several advantages of the use of an ePortfolio over a hard-copy portfolio, especially by contributing to creating opportunity for more deep learning. Their findings are shown in Table 1.1.

ePortfolios have several advantages over hard-copy portfolios. Not only do they save faculty members from carrying large, bulky notebooks across campus, they also have the potential to deepen student learning and transform the educational experience of students, faculty, and staff. If we help students in the process of developing their ePortfolios, they will have a concrete and visible way to capture their work over time, to scaffold their learning, and to connect their student experience from one assignment to another and one course to another, across programs and years.

THE EPORTFOLIO

As with any other online site, an ePortfolio allows readers to navigate, clicking on the areas they want to view. As readers move around the site, they might find definitions of the course's learning outcomes, links to work chosen to demonstrate progress or mastery, and reflective essays about how and why the work relates to the outcome.

You might also find ePortfolios with students' self-identified learning goals, sites that seem to be linked to particular courses, and others that might be directed at demonstrating one's learning to gain credit for prior learning. There is really no set architecture for an ePortfolio. The structure depends on the purpose and audience.

If you Google "student ePortfolios," you will find a variety of examples from different higher education institutions. In some, the work and reflection may appear insubstantial or lacking depth. These ePortfolios generally come from institutions where students create their own ePortfolios with little or no guidance from faculty or from the institution itself. Some institutions have ePortfolio labs staffed by student mentors that exist outside the curriculum and can be used for the students' own purposes or for the institution and in some cases for assessment.

Building an ePortfolio typically means that students employ the following process: collect, select, reflect, share or publish, get feedback. Students keep their work, which means that faculty, advisers, and staff should encourage students to develop the habit of saving their materials. Students can then select pieces that represent their progress or best work and then reflect on the samples they have chosen. In publishing or sharing their ePortfolios, students engage in a conversation about their work.

Students can follow this process in a number of ways. For example, if the ePortfolio is for a single course, students could

- save all their work from the beginning of the class,
- store the work in digital spaces,
- select specific work samples to demonstrate learning in specific learning outcomes,
- reflect on why they chose that work and how it demonstrates their learning in that outcome, and
- relate their learning across and beyond their academic experiences.

Of course, students can handle the ePortfolio process in several ways. Many students build their own portfolios with little or no institutional incentive or support. Perhaps they are interested in forging a digital identity or are interested in creating a space to share their work with family, friends, and colleagues. Most often, students first become involved in the ePortfolio process through some kind of institutional impetus, in other words as an assignment in a class, as a request from an academic adviser, or as a graduation requirement. Whatever the reason for starting an ePortfolio, students can benefit from the process of collect, select, reflect, and publish.

It is likely, and it is hoped, that students will be asked to build several ePortfolios throughout their years at an institution. Each of these portfolios can be seen as a *showcase* ePortfolio, designed for a particular purpose in a course or program. However, these portfolios can also be *working* or *process* ePortfolios that students continue to build on for different purposes and audiences. Once students have created one or more ePortfolios (especially if they are asked to throughout courses and programs and even their entire undergraduate or graduate years), they can build any number of showcase ePortfolios for any number of audiences.

In summary, ePortfolios are digital representations of students' work and accomplishments along with their reflections on their learning. The ePortfolio has the potential to enhance student learning through the process of collect, select, reflect, and share. In turn, the ePortfolio can provide authentic artifacts that aid in assessing student learning for student, program, and institutional purposes. ePortfolios can be self-initiated or directed and supported by institutional entities, such as faculty, staff, and university administrators. Finally, ePortfolios should not be seen as merely a snapshot of a student's work in time. ePortfolios have the potential to provide students with the opportunity to continue to document and reflect on their work throughout their educational experience and beyond. Students can create showcase ePortfolios for specific and multiple audiences and receive feedback.

INTEGRATIVE LEARNING EPORTFOLIOS

The beauty and the downfall of ePortfolios are that they are basically quite simple. One can actually create an ePortfolio in a manner of minutes, whether it is self-initiated or assigned. However, this brief interaction with one's work and web-based software will not likely lead to a deep or enlightening learning experience. As we began to create our own ePortfolio process at PSU and interacted with others using ePortfolios, we began to understand the diversity and differences in the depth of ePortfolios. Some institutions primarily focus on providing a digital repository of student work with little or no original content being added to the ePortfolio. At the other end of the continuum, other institutions require students to use the ePortfolio as a tool for helping students form their identities and for making connections between and beyond their course work. ePortfolios, of course, exist for different purposes and have different goals; their visual look and ways faculty and staff at institutions of higher education help students build them will be completely different. The types of ePortfolios are shown in Table 1.2.

As you can see, each point on the continuum makes sense if we consider the purpose and goals of a particular ePortfolio. For example, if your only goal is to provide a means for assessment of student work, an ePortfolio focused on content makes sense. If you are interested in helping students think about how and what they learned, a focus on content and the process of learning makes sense. Our focus, however, has been on creating integrative learning ePortfolios. As we discuss in Chapter 2, integrative learning has increasingly become an element in higher education. We explore integrative learning more in Chapter 2, but as you move to the right of Table 1.2, you can gain a sense of how much more complex the process becomes. Again, this book is designed to help you think through the process for creating integrative learning ePortfolios.

Table 1.2
Types of ePortfolios

Content Focused	Content and Process of Learning Focused	Content, Process, and Connections in Learning Focused	Integrative Learning
Artifacts/ demonstrations of learning	Artifacts/ demonstrations of learning	Artifacts/ demonstrations of learning	Artifacts/ demonstrations of learning
	Reflections on the artifacts	Reflections on the artifacts	Reflections on the artifacts
		Connections made between content in the ePortfolio	Connections made between content in the ePortfolio
			Use of the ePortfolio for identity development: connection between self and content of the ePortfolio

ePortfolios range from a simple electronic file cabinet to a rich sample of student work accompanied by student and faculty reflections on learning. In the creation of integrative learning ePortfolios, students can make sense of their work, their learning progress, and engage in self-evaluation, goal setting, and planning for the future. A substantive ePortfolio deepens learning and transforms the educational experience of students, faculty, and staff.

EXAMPLES OF EPORTFOLIOS

We thought it would be helpful to give you a few examples of what ePortfolios can look like. In this section, we present some examples of ePortfolios from a variety of institutions, each of which is clearly related to an institution's unique characteristics. None of these should be seen as the right way to think about building the architecture for an ePortfolio in your course or program but as inspiration for what is possible. The purposes of and audiences for these ePortfolios are different and we describe this briefly later. These examples are clearly not exhaustive of the wide variety of ePortfolios that exist in the academy. Links are provided if you want to learn more about these ePortfolio projects.

Portland State University

The University Studies Freshman Inquiry (Frinq) template used at PSU is shown in Figure 1.1, but the general format is common. The main focus of the Frinq ePortfolios

Figure 1.1
Freshman Inquiry Student ePortfolio Template

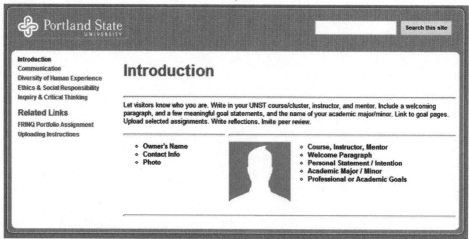

Note. From Portland State University, University Studies Program. Copyright 2014 by Portland State University, University Studies Program. Reproduced with permission.

is enhanced student learning, but the institution also uses those ePortfolios to assess the general education learning goals at the end of each year.

Introductory material is contained on the first page of an ePortfolio. This information can be in the form of a short essay we sometimes call a *learner autobiography*. This section gives the student a place to construct a personal portrait as a learner or as a professional. This activity at the entry level provides students who have not typically identified as college students, such as first-generation college students, a way to claim that identity and create a place for themselves at the university. The ePortfolio is organized by the general education goals for PSU, and these are listed in the navigation area on the left side of the screen. Readers can click on each goal to navigate to another page that includes the student's definition of the goal and a short reflection on why a specific work was chosen to represent that goal. The work sample, which demonstrates the student's level of competency, is linked to the goal page. The PSU ePortfolios also include reflections on learning that students write at the end of each term and a final reflection overview at the end of the year. The Freshman Inquiry ePortfolio is created in the first-year courses required by the university (e.g., see Figure 1.2). They are yearlong courses that include peer mentor sessions in small computer labs, thus allowing students an intentional experience with technology and substantial use of it in the curriculum. This template follows a common ePortfolio assignment that was created and adopted by the faculty who teach the Freshman Inquiry courses. PSU typically uses Google Sites, a free web application, to create ePortfolios, but students are allowed to use other software to create their ePortfolios. To view several student ePortfolios from PSU's University Studies program, go to https://sites.google.com/a/pdx.edu/eportresources/Home/ePortfolio-Showcase.

Figure 1.2
Freshman Inquiry ePortfolio Example

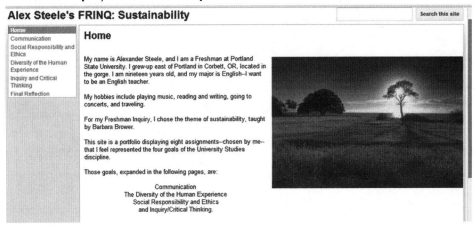

Figure 1.3
Master's Program Culminating ePortfolio

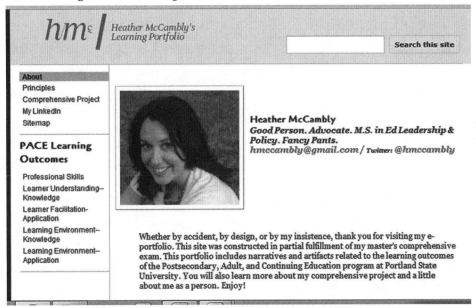

Several departments at PSU use ePortfolios. Candyce Reynolds's program in postsecondary adult and continuing education uses ePortfolios as the culminating project. The ePortfolio is centered on the learning outcomes of the program and provides evidence of student learning. It also asks students to develop and display their guiding principles of practice. Figure 1.3 is an example of a student's ePortfolio. See

Figure 1.4
Leadership ePortfolio Example

https://sites.google.com/a/pdx.edu/pace-comps-content for more information about the development process for ePortfolios in this program.

Also at PSU, student leaders participating in a leadership development program create an ePortfolio to help them articulate and demonstrate their understanding of the program's learning outcomes. Student leaders participate in a seminar and are expected to create ePortfolios. In the yearlong seminar, students meet several times a term, focusing on developing their philosophy page in the fall term. In the winter term, the focus is on developing pages on the learning outcomes of civility and diversity. In the spring term, students focus on a cohort-chosen learning outcome. In the example in Figure 1.4, the student focused on teamwork and also included her résumé and work samples.

LaGuardia Community College

LaGuardia ePortfolios include the following pages: Welcome, About Me, Classes and Projects, Educational Goals, Résumé, Links, and Contact Information. LaGuardia defines *ePortfolios* as

- An opportunity to effectively represent yourself and your education
- A place to collect and save coursework
- A chance to showcase accomplishments and school work to family and friends
- A tool for creating digital resumes to send to employers
- A web portal for accessing your work, track your academic growth and plan your career
- A portal that helps connect educational goals with personal experience

- An electronic resource you can use to apply for transfer and financial aid at a four year school
- A chance to reflect on your education, to make connections between where you are and where you want to be, and,
- A record of your skills, achievements and learning. (www.eportfolio.lagcc. cuny.edu/students/default.htm)

LaGuardia uses Digication, a web-based ePortfolio application available on Google campuses (i.e., campuses that have contracted with Google to provide e-mail and other online services via the Google Apps for Education suite) or for direct purchase from www.digication.com.

Clemson University

At Clemson University, undergraduate students are required to create an ePortfolio for graduation, such as the one shown in Figure 1.5.

> All undergraduates at Clemson University are expected to create and submit a digital portfolio as evidence of academic and experiential mastery of Clemson's core competencies. Students collect work from their classes and elsewhere, connecting (tagging) it to the competencies (Mathematical Literacy; Natural Science; Science and Technology in Society; Social Sciences; Cross-Cultural Awareness; Arts and Humanities; and the distributed competencies Ethical Judgment and Critical Thinking) throughout their undergraduate experience. The ePortfolio program was implemented in 2006 by Clemson University. The ePortfolio is a graduation requirement for ALL students; there are no exceptions. (Clemson University, n.d.a)

Figure 1.5
Clemson University Graduation ePortfolio Example

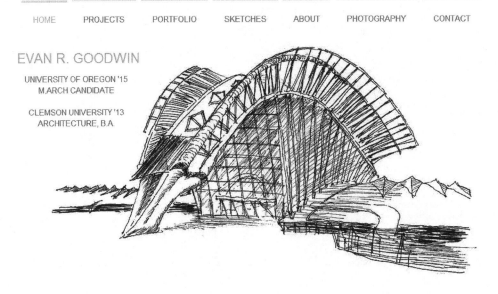

Clemson's definition of the ePortfolio includes information about what students should include:

> An ePortfolio is a collection of a student's work in electronic format. You should include a welcome/introduction to your ePortfolio. This is the first *virtual* impression that people will have of you, so make it a great one! You may even want to include a video welcome where you explain the organization of your ePortfolio and direct the viewer through the site. Your ePortfolio may contain all or some of the following:
>
> 1. Supporting files of various formats (text, pictures, video, etc.)
> 2. Evaluations, analysis and recommendations
> 3. Evidence of General Education competencies
> 4. Writing samples (which might include several drafts to show development and improvement)
> 5. Projects prepared for class or extracurricular activities
> 6. Evidence of creativity and performance
> 7. Evidence of extracurricular activities, including examples of leadership (Clemson University, n.d.b)

University of Michigan

At the University of Michigan, ePortfolios are used across the campus, from the business school to the chemistry department, from student affairs to the medical school. Called *MPortfolios*, they are defined as follows:

> MPortfolio is:
>
> - a process that enables students to reflect on and identify connections between their experiences inside and outside of the classroom;
> - a pedagogy that foregrounds substantial meaning-making and fosters intentional learning;
> - a product that illustrates a learner's development, knowledge, skills, and strengths; and
> - a team of people from around the University of Michigan campuses who are dedicated to integrative learning, information literacy, and student development.
>
> Students, staff, and faculty from many schools, colleges, and programs throughout the University of Michigan campuses are involved with MPortfolio, making up a strong community of learners and facilitators. Anyone at the University of Michigan can become involved with MPortfolio.
>
> The MPortfolio has many forms, one of which is the integrative knowledge ePortfolio. Developed by Melissa Peet and her colleagues in the School of Social Work, this type of ePortfolio enhances student learning; reveals the many ways in which Michigan students, faculty, and staff contribute to the public good;

and encourages students to create powerful connections between their experiences inside and outside of the classroom.

The Integrative Knowledge MPortfolio incorporates the following unique components:

- Valuing Learning From All Aspects of Life: Help students identify learning from all areas of their life, bridge their college experiences to other life experiences, and demonstrate how their underlying values and beliefs connect to their learning.
- Documenting Learning Beyond Graduation: Develop students' abilities to recognize "a-ha" moments in their lives and encourage them to document their knowledge, skills, and contributions beyond graduation.
- Understanding What We Know, Value, and Believe: Retrieving, reflecting, integrating, and documenting knowledge that has been gained through experience and connecting that knowledge to values, beliefs, and decision making.
- Supporting Assessment and Accountability: Students reflect on their learning, recognize how that learning relates to competencies, and demonstrate how those competencies inform their practice. (M. Peet, personal communication, July 18, 2011)

The showcase page and what students include in their ePortfolios are described as follows:

The portfolios presented here reflect the experiences of UM undergraduates from a range of educational levels, backgrounds and disciplines. The Integrative Knowledge Portfolio Process encourages students to ask questions essential for leadership and lifelong learning:

- Who am I becoming?
- What am I learning?
- What knowledge, skills and strengths am I developing?
- What can I do?
- How will I make a difference?

The portfolio process helps students approach problems strategically and collaboratively. Students learn to:

- Connect knowledge gained from real-life experiences and from academic courses
- Reflect on learning that has occurred both within and beyond the classroom
- Develop the knowledge, skills and awareness needed for professional competence and leadership
- Connect learning with personal values, a sense of purpose and goals for the future (M. Peet, personal communication, July 18, 2011)

Virginia Tech

Virginia Tech (2014) supports the development of ePortfolios across its departments and programs through its ePortfolio Initiatives:

> Electronic Portfolio Initiatives at Virginia Tech facilitates the use of electronic portfolios throughout the university. The ePortfolio project is an effort at improving education, learning assessment, and student engagement by using collaborative online tools that take advantage of the latest technology. ePortfolios offer ways to showcase individual skills, student learning, and professional development. The ePortfolio project is being coordinated by a team in Learning Technologies. (para. 1)

For more information about the initiative, see https://atel.tlos.vt.edu. The school provides a gallery of example ePortfolios that are used for learning, assessment, professional development, and cocurricular engagement.

Georgia Institute of Technology

One project that originated at Virginia Tech is a National Science Foundation grant aimed at helping engineering doctoral students at multiple institutions participate in an ePortfolio process that helps them move into the professoriate (the Portfolio to Professoriate program), with an emphasis on fostering reflective practice.

> Graduate engineering students at four universities around the country will create and maintain a portfolio focused on academic areas skills and experience such as teaching and research. Whether they [are] going into a teaching career or not, keeping a portfolio will provide numerous benefits to all participants, including a few valuable advantages when entering the job market. (Portfolio to Professoriate, n.d.)

Figure 1.6 is an example of one such ePortfolio by a Georgia Institute of Technology student. Note that the ePortfolio is organized using the same categories that those in the professoriate are judged on: teaching, research, and service.

Figure 1.6
Portfolio to Professoriate ePortfolio Example

Beyond College

ePortfolios are being used as people make the transition from the role of student to professional, often for the purpose of documenting lifelong learning and entry into the job market.

Wende Garrison, an ePortfolio maverick, started the Out of Practice group at the Association for Authentic, Experiential and Evidence-Based Learning conference to provide a support group for faculty and staff who advocated for student ePortfolios but did not maintain their own. Dozens of professionals have participated in workshops and online forums since the group's inception in 2010. Her portfolio (shown in Figure 1.7) is a great example of a lifelong learning ePortfolio and projects a professional but also personal digital identity to the world.

ePortfolios have the potential to be used as a vehicle for obtaining employment and provide employers with a dynamic view of an applicant. Students who have either used their student ePortfolios or continued to develop new ePortfolios to seek employment tell us that even if a potential employer never looks at the ePortfolio, they feel better prepared to represent their work in cover letters and interviews by going through the ePortfolio process. Our former student Slade Sapora is a good example of this. He continued to adapt and re-create ePortfolios after he graduated from the university, highlighting his work as a field biologist in Alaska and creating

Figure 1.7
Lifelong Learning ePortfolio Example

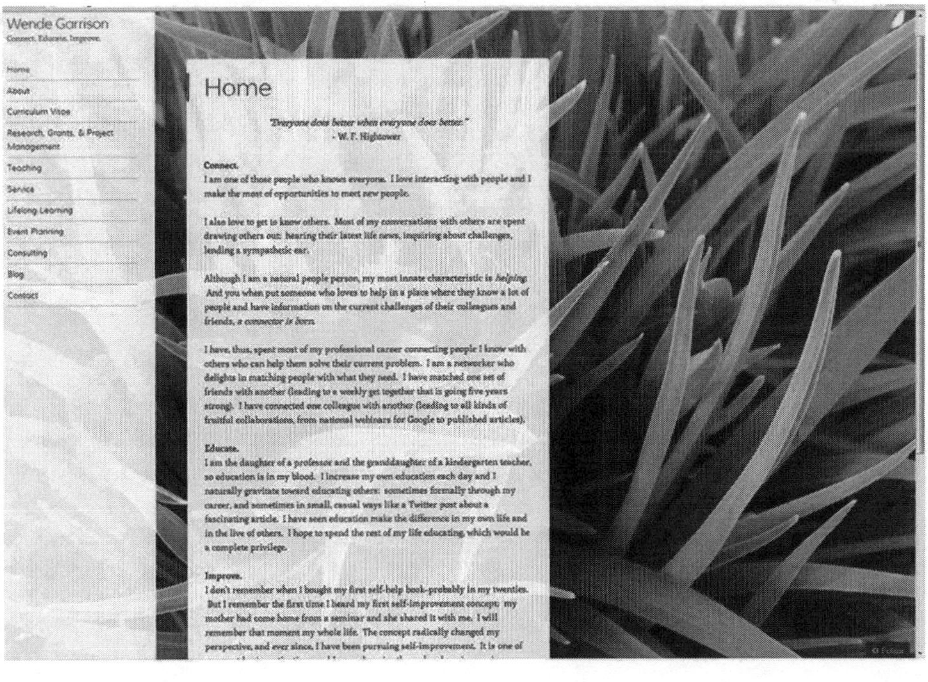

Figure 1.8
Employment ePortfolio Example

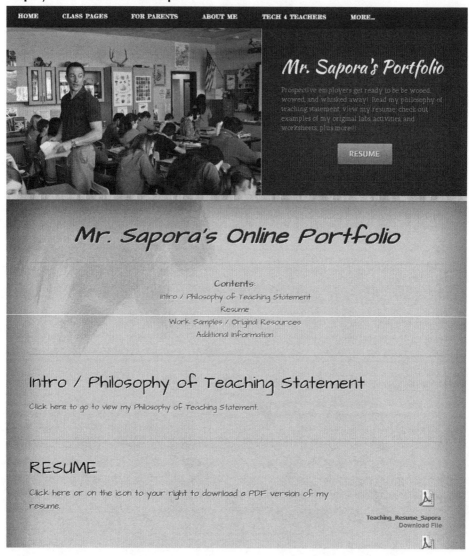

a portfolio of his photos for sale. Last year he developed an ePortfolio after graduating with an MS in education to use in seeking employment as a high school biology teacher. His ePortfolio, which helped him land his dream job, contains his résumé, teaching philosophy, and a diverse set of resources and work samples (see Figure 1.8). He plans to continue to develop and expand his ePortfolio and put much of the work it contains to use in his new classroom.

These different ePortfolios show us that each institution has developed a process and template that fits the student experience it wishes to provide. We cannot stress enough how vital it is for each institution to determine the uses of ePortfolios for its specific environment and take time to ask faculty, staff, and students what they want to include and be able to do with the ePortfolio before any decision about software or platforms is made. When ePortfolios are part of a planned curriculum, a process of its design and creation is part of its use, and the benefits of this process are many.

BACKGROUND AND LEARNING CONTEXT FOR EPORTFOLIOS

The most convincing reasons for using learning ePortfolios come from research on learning, on how the brain works, and on motivation. The concept of transformational learning comes from the work of Jack Mezirow. In an overview article of the theory, E.W. Taylor (2007) explains:

> Mezirow does not see transformative learning as an "add-on" educational practice or technique. He sees it as the very essence of adult education, such that the goal of adult education is "to help the individual become a more autonomous thinker by learning to negotiate his or her own values, meanings, and purpose rather than uncritically acting on those of others" (Mezirow 1997, p. 11). . . . Significant learning involves the transformation of meaning structures through an ongoing process of critical reflection, discourse, and acting on one's beliefs. (Taylor, 2007, p. 12)

In higher education, we lament that while we strive to produce graduates who are self-directed learners and autonomous thinkers, we often fall short in these efforts. Ryan and Deci's (2000) research finds that when we do something because it is inherently enjoyable or interesting or intrinsically motivating, we produce higher quality learning. Environments in which students experience a sense of competence, autonomy, and relatedness especially nurture good learning and foster intrinsic motivation. Students experience competence when challenged and given prompt feedback.

> Students experience autonomy when they feel supported to explore, take initiative and develop and implement solutions for their problems. Students experience relatedness when they perceive others listening and responding to them. When these three needs are met, students are more intrinsically motivated and actively engaged in their learning. (Ryan & Deci, 2000, Findings section, para. 1)

Research on learning and the brain (e.g., Bransford, Brown, & Cocking, 1999; Halpern & Hakel, 2000; Tagg, 2004; Zull, 2002) supports the idea that we need to teach for one goal: long-term learning with the ability to apply that learning. To achieve that goal, faculty must know where students are in their understanding of the content area, and students need to understand how learning actually happens. In constructing learning experiences, students need to be asked to retrieve information many times in differing situations and contexts and also to learn and then re-represent information in different formats, such as listening and writing, then re-represent that in a visual or spatial manner, and vice versa. Faculty need to design their courses around the concept of less is more. If we want students to *understand* and be able to use material, we need to spend more time on significant concepts and cover less material. Chickering and Gamson (1987) said students "must talk about what they are learning, write about it, relate it to past experiences, and apply it to their daily lives. They must make what they learn part of themselves" (p. 4). Halpern and Hakel (2000) state it this way:

> What learners do determines what and how much is learned, how well it will be remembered, and the conditions under which it will be recalled. Our most important role as teachers is to direct learning activities in ways that maximize long-term retention and transfer. What professors do in their classes matters far less than what they ask *students* to do. (p. 41)

ePortfolios, then, as a pedagogical tool, offer rich opportunities to engage students by leveraging the practices we know promote deep learning. Using ePortfolios in our work with students asks them to save their work over time, mine that work by looking for and evaluating their own progress, connect their learning from assignment to assignment and course to course, reflect upon and record what they have learned and how they have learned it, and set goals for the future. Most important, ePortfolios are a living document, a discussion, if you will, between the student and teacher, student and colleagues, student and the world. Students can create an ePortfolio in groups, sharing ideas, talents, and critiques, and determining standards based on real peer work and evidence in work of excellence in diverse fields. Part Two of this book further explores the pedagogical practices involved in using ePortfolios in your classroom or program.

Chapter 2

Integrating Knowledge
The Crux of an Education

Candyce's Story: The bad—Yet another essay turned in that seems to ignore all of what my students have studied (or so I thought) over a whole term. We have discussed the concepts repeatedly; they have written papers and have been given detailed feedback. But again, a significant number of my students have minimally answered the question posed for their final paper and completely ignored my instructions to synthesize materials from the whole class as well as from their earlier psychology courses. They seemed to only pay attention to what is right in front of them—what they studied last week—and missed out on the bigger picture: how it all fits together. The good—I was looking forward to seeing my Freshman Inquiry students' final ePortfolios, but I was actually surprised to see what my students had done. Many seemed to have learned what I had hoped they had learned, and many had learned more than I could have imagined by making connections beyond the scope of the course. One student summed it up nicely in his reflection about the program's critical thinking goal:

I have always heard that school was about increasing your critical thinking skills. It was the mantra throughout my life. Of course, I was learning critical thinking and, of course, I WAS a critical thinker. However, it wasn't until this class that I had a true understanding of what critical thinking is and why it might be important. Having to define critical thinking for myself and putting together this portfolio made me realize what it really is and how little I actually know about how to do it. Now I see critical thinking everywhere I look. I need to use it with my roommate when we are figuring out how we are going to divide our bills—and it isn't about the money! I need it to make decisions at work and in my personal life. I need it in my other classes. The mantra was right, but I didn't really understand it. I'm only beginning to now and I hope I'll be developing this important skill as I get older and wiser.

This student was able to make connections between what he had learned in the past, what he is learning now, and what he hopes to learn in the future. He has learned across boundaries, school, work, and play. He is on the road to experiencing integrative learning.

Integrative learning such as this is necessary for us to be successful in our complex world. We need to integrate our learning throughout our lives. Not too long ago, I was asked to chair a committee to look at faculty issues related to online learning practices on our campus. I had a few twinges of apprehension, but at the heart of it, I knew that I could work through the kinks I might encounter addressing this complex issue. My ability to tackle this assignment is a testament to the ability to integrate previous learning and put into action what is known. To fill the role, I needed to draw from a myriad of skills, knowledge, and experiences. I used my knowledge from my own experience and research on online learning. The knowledge I needed came not only from my current experiences but also from seemingly random places, such as my most hated course on learning I took as an undergraduate that seemed irrelevant at the time. And who knew that being on the debate team in middle school would have contributed to my delivering the concluding report to the Faculty Senate? That is what integrative learning is all about: having the ability to pull together what appears to be disparate knowledge and skills and make them into a new, unified whole.

While we would probably all agree that integrative learning is a necessary part of education, especially higher education, there is little agreement about how to make this happen. In discussions regarding integrative learning in higher education, one controversial issue is when and how this kind of learning should happen. Some argue that integrative learning occurs only after students have acquired base knowledge, others might contend that integrative learning needs to be addressed early and often, and many faculty we encounter in office hallways even maintain that this isn't the purview of faculty at all. They argue that integrative learning is innate and cannot and should not be taught, or, at a minimum, that students need to do it on their own. Our view is that we need to model and make explicit in our teaching practices the process of integrative learning, something that happens all the time. Without the ability to integrate our moment-to-moment experiences, we would be at a loss in managing our lives. As faculty, we just need to put ourselves in the midst of the integrative learning that is already happening in our students and make sure that what we are teaching gets in the mix. We show how integrative learning ePortfolios can help ensure this connection.

This chapter provides an overview of current thinking regarding integrative learning, starting with definitions, followed by a discussion of why integrative learning is an important learning outcome especially in higher education. The chapter ends with a discussion of the Association of American Colleges and Universities' (AAC&U) integrative learning rubric (Rhodes, 2010).

INTEGRATIVE LEARNING

All learning is integrative learning. We thrive in the world because we are able to make connections between what we have learned in the past to what we are learning in the future. Integrative learning, at the crux, is the ability to learn across context and over time and to be motivated to learn this way.

Learning how to add numbers in kindergarten builds the skills necessary for us to do multiplication in later grades. When we are faced with solving a multiplication or division problem, we can call up and use the knowledge we have about addition to help us solve our current problem. Likewise, when we learn to tie our first knot, that skill allows us to learn how to tie our shoes. Becoming a Boy Scout or Girl Scout also provides the opportunity to learn to tie even more complicated knots. One can argue that learning to tie knots actually set us up to learn other skills that require hand-eye coordination, like writing out the alphabet or threading a needle. Learning historical facts can also prepare us for learning and understanding deeply historical or current happenings. For example, remembering when and why World War I was fought can help us understand the conditions that brought about World War II as well as help us understand current issues in Europe and the world. And we make even more connections when we know someone who experienced the war and when we look at the artwork from that time. In these examples, we can see that integrative learning entails the ability to use prior knowledge and experience and build on that knowledge (the over time part) and to use our knowledge and experience in different situations (the across context part).

Integrative learning also entails seeing one's self as an active agent in one's life. To be able to engage in integrative learning, one must seek to see connections. In reality, connections are always there; we just don't always see them. Seeing oneself as a learner—motivated and capable of putting ideas together—is an important part of using integrative learning. Having the habit of mind that engenders curiosity propels us to ask questions and seek answers to questions such as, how does World War I relate to World War II? Learning one knot and then another leads you to want to learn to tie even more complicated knots. However, garnering this motivation or a habit of mind is not an easy task. Dunlap and Sult (2009) use the analogy of juggling in describing learning, reporting that they both require "simultaneous manipulation and integration of multiple objects (or concepts and processes) into a purposeful pattern" (p. 27). While juggling can be fun, it can also be intimidating. To grapple with the often difficult task of putting ideas together, one must be willing to engage and learn through trial and error, and risk dropping the ball. Integrative learning requires students to be motivated and intentional in their efforts to learn.

Huber and Hutchings (2004) explain integrative learning as follows:

> One of the great challenges in higher education is to foster students' abilities to integrate their learning across contexts and over time. . . . The capacity to connect is central . . . whether focused on discovery and creativity, integrating and interpreting knowledge from disciplines, [or] applying knowledge through real-world engagements. (p. 1)

> [An] emphasis on integrative learning can help undergraduates put the pieces together and develop habits of mind that prepare them to make informed judgments in the conduct of personal, professional, and civic life. (p. 13)

Carol Schneider (2003), president of AAC&U, also defines *integrative learning*:

> Integrative learning is a shorthand term for teaching a set of capacities—capacities we might also call the arts of connection, reflective judgment, and considered action—that enable graduates to put their knowledge to effective

use. . . . It should also lead students to connect and integrate the different parts of their overall education, to connect learning with the world beyond the academy, and, above all, to translate their education to new contexts, new problems, new responsibilities. (pp. 1–2)

So at its essence, integrative learning means that we learn things and are able to figure out how to use these things again in the future or in different situations, and it entails the development of one's self as an intentional learner able to determine when and how to use the knowledge and skills one has gained. Integrative learning can be summarized in this general formula:

Integrative learning = learning over time + learning across context + intention

We propose that the concept of surface and deep learning is related to the concept of integrative learning. While common sense tells us that learning is certainly not this clearly dichotomous, the concepts are helpful in thinking about our goals for higher education. Surface learning occurs when students focus their attention on what is needed to pass a particular class. Students engage minimally with the content of the course and tend to see what is being learned as discrete pieces of information that are unrelated to other things they have learned in the past as well as things they might need in the future. Deep learning, on the other hand, occurs when students engage more fully with the content. They seek out underlying principles and consider ways to connect with what they have learned before and what they might be able to use in the future. Thus, surface learning focuses on discrete pieces of information, and deep learning focuses on making connections. Of course we want our students to intentionally employ deep learning strategies with the goal of being able to integrate their knowledge. However, our practices in higher education do not necessarily align with this ultimate goal, which we explore in the next section.

INTEGRATIVE LEARNING IN HIGHER EDUCATION

While the term *integrative learning* may be relatively new in the higher education landscape, it is nonetheless the primary goal of education, whether stated as such or not. The long-recognized purpose of higher education has been to educate the whole student, not just contribute to a student's intellectual development but also foster personal understanding and fulfillment and an ability and desire to contribute to the larger societal whole. As S. H. Taylor (2011) says, students should graduate with "a more sophisticated way of knowing and interacting with the world" (p. 15). Unfortunately, our educational systems don't always support our avowed purposes. In fact, it can sometimes seem that our institutions of higher education are designed to thwart integrative learning or encourage surface learning over deep learning. From high school (and probably even earlier), students are taught that knowledge in the context of a *subject* or a *course*. And this discussion doesn't even include what students might know and learn outside the classroom, experiences that are often treated as if they don't matter or are not part of one's learning and development. What one knows and learns at home often seems disconnected to what one learns and knows in school.

In institutions of higher education, disciplines reign. Our students get degrees in history, English, psychology, and business administration. Most of our institutions are structured this way, and while they require courses outside the major to provide a *liberal* education, students and faculty alike understand that the discipline is the most important. You could almost say that we beat the natural tendency toward integrative learning out of our students through our relentless focus on the disciplines. Students and faculty are both rewarded for their understanding and advancement in the discipline. It should not be surprising, then, when those of us in academia are confronted with critiques of higher education, such as those found in *Academically Adrift: Limited Learning on College Campuses* (Arum & Roksa, 2011), that claim our students are not learning enough or not learning what they should be learning in higher education. In our pursuit to help students learn the discipline of history or psychology, we have forgotten that college has a broader purpose. We must not only educate for knowledge of facts and ideas but also teach how to put those ideas together and apply them to pressing problems of the day and in the future. Integrative learning is actually an essential skill.

In fact, leaders in higher education have begun to acknowledge the importance of fostering integrative learning in our students and call for changes in the way we teach. The Carnegie Foundation for the Advancement of Teaching and the AAC&U teamed up in the middle of the first decade of the 21st century in a project that brought together innovative campus leaders to explore integrative learning in higher education. One result of this work was the groundbreaking publication *Liberal Education and America's Promise* (AAC&U, 2007b). This document identified integrative and applied learning as one of four essential learning outcomes of college, along with knowledge of human cultures and the physical and natural world, intellectual and practical skills (e.g., communication and creative and critical thinking), and personal and social responsibility. The publication also identified high-impact practices for achieving these learning outcomes, which include such diverse activities as first-year seminars, writing-intensive courses, and service-learning. Not surprisingly, as of late ePortfolios have emerged as a high-impact practice especially for achieving integrative learning (e.g., Chen & Penny Light, 2010).

AAC&U (n.d.) has also sought to help our institutions define and assess these learning outcomes through the Valid Assessment of Learning in Undergraduate Education (VALUE) project.

> As part of the VALUE project, diverse teams of faculty and other academic and student affairs professionals from a wide range of institutions drafted and revised institutional-level rubrics (and related materials) to correspond with the AAC&U Essential Learning Outcomes. Each VALUE rubric (listed below) contains the most broadly shared criteria or core characteristics considered to be critical for judging the quality of student work in a particular outcome area.

Intellectual and Practical Skills

- Inquiry and analysis
- Critical thinking
- Creative thinking
- Written communication
- Oral communication
- Reading
- Quantitative literacy
- Information literacy
- Teamwork
- Problem solving

Personal and Social Responsibility

- Civic knowledge and engagement—local and global
- Intercultural knowledge and competence
- Ethical reasoning
- Foundations and skills for lifelong learning
- Global Learning

Integrative and Applied Learning

- Integrative and applied learning

Faculty and staff can use the integrative learning rubric to help develop activities that facilitate integrative learning and to assess it. The team that developed the following rubric defines *integrative learning* as "an understanding and a disposition that a student builds across the curriculum and co-curriculum, from making simple connections among ideas and experiences to synthesizing and transferring learning to new, complex situations within and beyond the campus" (see Exhibit 2.1). The rubric identifies ways that integrative learning can be demonstrated through student work and provides a framework for judging the quality of the work through these categories:

- Connection to Experience: Connects relevant experience and academic knowledge
- Connection to Discipline: Sees (makes) connections across disciplines, perspectives
- Transfer: Adapts and applies skills, abilities, theories, or methodologies gained in one situation to new situations
- Integrated Communication: The presentation of material that represents appropriate types of communication, including visuals, and takes into consideration audience
- Reflection and Self-Assessment: Demonstrates a developing sense of self as a learner, building on prior experiences to respond to new and challenging contexts.

For this rubric for integrative learning, along with the other VALUE rubrics, see www.aacu.org/value/rubrics/index_p.cfm?CFID=13089876&CFTOKEN=61143662.

Exhibit 2.1
Integrative Learning VALUE Rubric

The VALUE rubrics were developed by teams of faculty experts representing colleges and universities across the United States through a process that examined many existing campus rubrics and related documents for each learning outcome and incorporated additional feedback from faculty. The rubrics articulate fundamental criteria for each learning outcome, with performance descriptors demonstrating progressively more sophisticated levels of attainment. The rubrics are intended for institutional-level use in evaluating and discussing student learning, not for grading. The core expectations articulated in all 15 of the VALUE rubrics can and should be translated into the language of individual campuses, disciplines, and even courses. The utility of the VALUE rubrics is to position learning at all undergraduate levels within a basic framework of expectations such that evidence of learning can be shared nationally through a common dialog and understanding of student success.

DEFINITION

Integrative learning is an understanding and a disposition that a student builds across the curriculum and co-curriculum, from making simple connections among ideas and experiences to synthesizing and transferring learning to new, complex situations within and beyond the campus.

FRAMING LANGUAGE

Fostering students' abilities to integrate learning—across courses, over time, and between campus and community life—is one of the most important goals and challenges for higher education. Initially, students connect previous learning to new classroom learning. Later, significant knowledge within individual disciplines serves as the foundation, but integrative learning goes beyond academic boundaries. Indeed, integrative experiences often occur as learners address real-world problems, unscripted and sufficiently broad, to require multiple areas of knowledge and multiple modes of inquiry, offering multiple solutions and benefiting from multiple perspectives. Integrative learning also involves internal changes in the learner. These internal changes, which indicate growth as a confident, lifelong learner, include the ability to adapt one's intellectual skills, to contribute in a wide variety of situations, and to understand and develop individual purpose, values and ethics. Developing students' capacities for integrative

learning is central to personal success, social responsibility, and civic engagement in today's global society. Students face a rapidly changing and increasingly
connected world where integrative learning becomes not just a benefit... but
a necessity.

Because integrative learning is about making connections, this learning may not be as evident in traditional academic artifacts such as research
papers and academic projects unless the student, for example, is prompted
to draw implications for practice. These connections often surface, however,
in reflective work, self assessment, or creative endeavors of all kinds. Integrative assignments foster learning between courses or by connecting courses to
experientially-based work. Work samples or collections of work that include
such artifacts give evidence of integrative learning. Faculty are encouraged to
look for evidence that the student connects the learning gained in classroom
study to learning gained in real life situations that are related to other learning
experiences, extra-curricular activities, or work. Through integrative learning,
students pull together their entire experience inside and outside of the formal classroom; thus, artificial barriers between formal study and informal or
tacit learning become permeable. Integrative learning, whatever the context or
source, builds upon connecting both theory and practice toward a deepened
understanding.

Assignments to foster such connections and understanding could include,
for example, composition papers that focus on topics from biology, economics,
or history; mathematics assignments that apply mathematical tools to important
issues and require written analysis to explain the implications and limitations of
the mathematical treatment, or art history presentations that demonstrate aes-
thetic connections between selected paintings and novels. In this regard, some
majors (e.g., interdisciplinary majors or problem-based field studies) seem to
inherently evoke characteristics of integrative learning and result in work samples or collections of work that significantly demonstrate this outcome. However, fields of study that require accumulation of extensive and high-consensus
content knowledge (such as accounting, engineering, or chemistry) also involve
the kinds of complex and integrative constructions (e.g., ethical dilemmas and
social consciousness) that seem to be highlighted so extensively in self reflection
in arts and humanities, but they may be embedded in individual performances
and less evident. The key in the development of such work samples or collections of work will be in designing structures that include artifacts and reflective
writing or feedback that support students' examination of their learning and
give evidence that, as graduates, they will extend their integrative abilities into
the challenges of personal, professional, and civic life.

GLOSSARY

The definitions that follow were developed to clarify terms and concepts used in this rubric only.

- Academic knowledge: Disciplinary learning; learning from academic study, texts, etc.
- Content: The information conveyed in the work samples or collections of work.
- Contexts: Actual or simulated situations in which a student demonstrates learning outcomes. New and challenging contexts encourage students to stretch beyond their current frames of reference.
- Co-curriculum: A parallel component of the academic curriculum that is in addition to formal classroom (student government, community service, residence hall activities, student organizations, etc.).
- Experience: Learning that takes place in a setting outside of the formal classroom, such as workplace, service learning site, internship site or another.
- Form: The external frameworks in which information and evidence are presented, ranging from choices for particular work sample or collection of works (such as a research paper, PowerPoint, video recording, etc.) to choices in make-up of the eportfolio.
- Performance: A dynamic and sustained act that brings together knowing and doing (creating a painting, solving an experimental design problem, developing a public relations strategy for a business, etc.); performance makes learning observable.
- Reflection: A meta-cognitive act of examining a performance in order to explore its significance and consequences.
- Self Assessment: Describing, interpreting, and judging a performance based on stated or implied expectations followed by planning for further learning.

DEFINITION

Integrative learning is an understanding and a disposition that a student builds across the curriculum and cocurriculum, from making simple connections among ideas and experiences to synthesizing and transferring learning to new, complex situations within and beyond the campus.

Evaluators are encouraged to assign a zero to any work sample or collection of work that does not meet benchmark (cell one) level performance.

	Capstone 4	Milestones 3	Milestones 2	Benchmark 1
Connections to Experience *Connects relevant experience and academic knowledge*	Meaningfully **synthesizes** connections among experiences outside of the formal classroom (including life experiences and academic experiences such as internships and travel abroad) to **deepen understanding** of fields of study and to broaden own points of view.	Effectively **selects and develops** examples of life experiences, drawn from a variety of contexts (e.g., family life, artistic participation, civic involvement, work experience), to **illuminate** concepts/theories/frameworks of fields of study.	**Compares** life experiences and academic knowledge to infer differences, as well as similarities, and **acknowledge perspectives** other than own.	**Identifies** connections between life experiences and those academic texts and ideas **perceived as similar and related** to own interests.
Connections to Discipline *Sees (makes) connections across disciplines, perspectives*	Independently creates wholes out of multiple parts (synthesizes) or draws conclusions by combining examples, facts, or theories from more than one field of study or perspective.	Independently connects examples, facts, or theories from more than one field of study or perspective.	When prompted, connects examples, facts, or theories from more than one field of study or perspective.	When prompted, presents examples, facts, or theories from more than one field of study or perspective.
Transfer *Adapts and applies skills, abilities, theories, or methodologies gained in one situation to new situations*	Adapts and applies, independently, skills, abilities, theories, or methodologies gained in one situation to new situations **to solve difficult problems or explore complex issues in original ways.**	Adapts and applies skills, abilities, theories, or methodologies gained in one situation to new situations **to solve problems or explore issues.**	Uses skills, abilities, theories, or methodologies gained in one situation in a new situation **to contribute to understanding of problems or issues.**	Uses, in a basic way, skills, abilities, theories, or methodologies gained in one situation **in a new situation.**

	Capstone 4	Milestones 3	Milestones 2	Benchmark 1
Integrated Communication	Fulfills the assignment(s) by choosing a format, language, or graph (or other visual representation) **in ways that enhance meaning**, making clear the interdependence of language and meaning, thought, and expression.	Fulfills the assignment(s) by choosing a format, language, or graph (or other visual representation) **to explicitly connect content and form**, demonstrating awareness of purpose and audience.	Fulfills the assignment(s) by choosing a format, language, or graph (or other visual representation) that **connects in a basic way** what is being communicated (content) with how it is said (form).	Fulfills the assignment(s) (i.e. to produce an essay, a poster, a video, a PowerPoint presentation, etc.) **in an appropriate form.**
Reflection and Self-Assessment *Demonstrates a developing sense of self as a learner, building on prior experiences to respond to new and challenging contexts (may be evident in self-assessment, reflective, or creative work)*	Envisions a future self (and possibly makes plans that build on past experiences) that have occurred across multiple and diverse contexts.	Evaluates changes in own learning over time, recognizing complex contextual factors (e.g., works with ambiguity and risk, deals with frustration, considers ethical frameworks).	Articulates strengths and challenges (within specific performances or events) to increase effectiveness in different contexts (through increased self-awareness).	Describes own performances with general descriptors of success and failure.

Note. From *Assessing Outcomes and Improving Achievement: Tips and Tools for Using Rubrics*, edited by T. L. Rhodes, 2010, Washington, DC: Association of American Colleges and Universities. Copyright 2010 by Association of American Colleges and Universities. Reprinted with permission.

ALIGNING OUR INTENTIONS FOR INTEGRATIVE LEARNING

Because integrative learning is so central to the goals of higher education, and at the same time so deeply discouraged in practice, faculty must reprioritize the development of integrative learning in their classrooms. Changing curricular structures and the organization of higher education to more directly foster integrative learning is unlikely to happen very soon. But as individual faculty members, we can certainly refocus our attention on educating for integrative learning. This book focuses on classroom practices that facilitate integrative learning using the ePortfolio as a tool.

The concepts of surface and deep learning come into play directly with ePortfolios. While surface and deep learning are characteristics of students' approach to learning, the reality is that we encourage or discourage deep learning, and thus integrative learning, by what we do in our classrooms, what we focus on in the classroom, and what rewards we bestow in our student assessment and grading practices. Too often we ask our students to regurgitate facts and ideas without asking them to make deeper connections beyond what they are learning in one particular classroom. A focus on integrative learning calls for us to look at our own classroom practices and consider how we help our students make these connections.

TEACHING FOR INTEGRATIVE LEARNING USING EPORTFOLIOS: SOME GENERAL PRINCIPLES

We hope by now that you are encouraged by the good news that integrative learning is a natural process and that our students are capable of engaging in it fully. Often we just don't ask them to make those connections, and they get out of practice. And it is our hope that by asking them to participate in deep learning processes, including the creation of an ePortfolio, you can facilitate that process. In Chapter 3 we talk about how to integrate integrative learning into your courses, and in Part Two we focus on applying learning theory to practical strategies for you to use in your classrooms or programs. To help frame these discussions and close our discussion in this chapter, we first want to share some broader principles that have guided our work in integrative learning through ePortfolios.

Our students are adults; treat them as such. While we should acknowledge that our students are often on the cusp of adulthood, it does neither us nor them any good to treat them as if they were children. We find it useful to consider the characteristics that Malcolm Knowles (1980) recognized in adult learners. He argued that adults have life experiences, and they bring those experiences to the classroom. To ignore those experiences and the knowledge they have gained is to cut off an opportunity to integrate that learning with what is being examined in your classroom. Adults are inherently goal oriented, self-directed, and practical. Learning for learning's sake is a virtuous goal, but as adults we often don't have time to ponder anything beyond our immediate needs. Helping students connect what they are learning in your classroom to the things that matter to them most will motivate them.

Make the learning relevant. As faculty and staff, we have a lot of control over the conditions that influence integrative learning, but the one thing we can't do is make someone learn something. Learning requires attention, which is related to motivation. I can hear what most people would consider a fantastic lecture or read a passage from my statistics textbook and not be able to recall or apply any of the material if I have not made the effort to pay attention. I can physically do the work that is asked of me, but that does not mean that I've learned it. (This is one reason why we think it is important to give points or credit for participation in class and not for attendance.) To make connections between ideas over time and context, we need to pay attention and make the effort for this to happen.

Some of this has to do with motivation, of course. We pay attention to what we believe to be important or at the very least is interesting to us. Often motivation starts from within. This is what we hope for in the classroom. We can become interested in something when we see that it is related, or we can make a connection to our past knowledge. I get interested in the lecture on Homer's *Odyssey* because I see a connection between the ideas being talked about and the story line in my favorite movie, *Star Wars*. Being able to relate something new to something I already understand and care about motivates me to pay attention. The act of making these kinds of connections is fun and enjoyable, and it can happen with ease. But motivation doesn't necessarily start from within. Sometimes motivation, and thus our attention, first starts outside ourselves. I pay attention to the lecture because I want to pass the test that is coming next week. In the process of listening and studying, I start to see how the material falls together with material that was presented earlier in the course, and I may even start to see how it relates to the course I took last term or maybe even something I learned in Girl Scouts many years ago.

So for integrative learning to happen for our students, they need to pay attention and start to make connections between what is happening now and what has come before. We can provide lots of information and even glitzy productions, but without the motivation to pay attention, the learning that happens may be short-lived. Whether the motivation to pay attention comes first from within or comes first from outside oneself, relevance is the key.

Make the process of learning active. For integrative learning to happen, students need to engage actively with the material. Simply put, integrative learning will not take place if we do not get our hands dirty in putting ideas together. It is easy enough to memorize facts and regurgitate them for a final test. This is a clear logical progression: The input goes into the student and the output emerges relatively unchanged. What happens in between the lecture and the test is a simple process of memorization. Integrative learning, on the other hand, requires multiple inputs, and the outputs from students may look similar, but they will not be exactly the same. What happens in between is the stuff of creativity and individualism. To foster integrative learning, we must invite our students to bring in ideas from multiple sources, get confused, and make mistakes. That way, they will understand that there are no easy answers.

CHAPTER 3

Retooling Your Syllabus and Teaching

Integrating Integrative Learning and ePortfolios Into Your Course

Judy and Candyce's story: At the end of every academic year, faculty from across campus come together to review ePortfolios from our first-year Freshman Inquiry for program assessment. Many students are able to demonstrate their learning through quality reflections and artifacts far beyond what many faculty would expect from first-year students. Such ePortfolios typically spark faculty curiosity. How were the students able to do it? Did our incoming students get brighter? On exploration, the reality becomes clear: Those students who demonstrate the best learning were in Freshman Inquiry courses where the faculty has carefully developed activities and assignments that allow them to practice and then demonstrate their learning. (By the way, doing program assessment in this way is a very effective faculty development activity. Seeing excellent student work motivates faculty to learn what they can do to achieve similar outcomes.)

Understanding the importance of integrative learning for students and how effective ePortfolios can be in facilitating the process is just the beginning. Now comes the hard part—implementing this in your classroom or in an academic or cocurricular program. This chapter discusses establishing learning outcomes in your course or program and strategies that provide opportunities to help students make connections between and beyond them. We also discuss establishing integrative learning goals as well as provide a framework for integrating these learning outcomes into your courses, focusing specifically on creating ePortfolio assignments. Last, we discuss how to balance integrative learning outcomes with your course or program content outcomes.

INTEGRATIVE LEARNING AS A COURSE GOAL

Everyone is for integrative learning. It is kind of like a chocolate chip cookie at the end of the meal—what's not to like? However, someone has to make the chocolate chip cookie and bring that plateful of cookies to the table. Simply saying you believe in integrative learning and promote it in your courses does not mean that it happens on its own. As an instructor, you need to make integrative learning an actual goal of your course and provide opportunities for your students to participate in the process of making connections.

Incorporating an ePortfolio assignment into your course design is one way to make integrative learning a transparent learning goal for your students. An integrative learning ePortfolio assignment makes it clear to students that making connections is an important part of learning in your course. ePortfolios are typically assigned as a culminating activity for students. And while they may be finished at the end of a course, it is imperative to include activities that promote integrative learning and that contribute to the development of the ePortfolio throughout your course. As with any skill we develop, integrative learning requires practice. Part Two (Chapters 4–7) focuses on specific activities supported by learning theories that help students develop integrative learning skills and can be incorporated into your course design.

Incorporating integrative learning into your course or program can happen many ways. You can ask students to integrate their learning through an ePortfolio using the strategies we discuss in Part Two. In addition, you can define specific integrative learning outcomes in your course, or you can do both. However you do it, we are proposing that you make integrative learning a central outcome of your course. Well-written learning outcomes for a course and especially those directed at integrative learning provide students with many benefits, including the following:

- Students have a clearer understanding of what is important in the course. Students often come to a course with little background information on the subject of your course. Even if they have some background, they don't necessarily understand how the content fits together and what is most important. Learning outcomes can help students focus on what is most important about a subject. If integrating one's knowledge is a prominent learning outcome, students will know this is an important area to focus on.
- Students have a clearer understanding of what is expected of them. When learning outcomes are written clearly and specifically, students know what they need to do in the course to get that good grade but also what they need to do to become proficient in that field of study. If integrative learning is identified as a learning outcome, students can begin to see that just learning facts about a topic is not enough; making connections and applying these facts is at least equally if not more important in mastering a field of study.
- Students have the language for the process of integrative learning, which can facilitate continuing to make these connections in other settings. Because students may not have been exposed directly to the concept of integrative learning in their previous studies, they may not have paid attention or given much credit to the fact that they were making connections between the course content and their workplace, for example. Integrative learning has often taken on the status of bonus learning for students, if they've even recognized it as learning. Naming integrative learning as a course goal allows students to start

to see the importance of being able to make connections and encourages them to continue making these connections.

- Students are better able to self-assess; they can use the learning outcomes to measure what they have learned in a course. Learning outcomes provide a great opportunity for students to look back on a course or program and evaluate their progress, asking themselves, What did I master? What do I need to spend a bit more time on? This kind of self-assessment for integrative learning outcomes can prompt students to push even further in making connections with what they've learned in the course.

Faculty also reap the following benefits from well-written learning outcomes:

- Learning outcomes help faculty organize and develop learning activities aimed at helping students achieve these outcomes. Learning outcomes provide the road map for course planning. Course descriptions and outlines give us information about what we should cover in a course, but learning outcomes help us to be able to think deeply about what we want our students to learn in our courses. Developing integrative learning outcomes guides faculty in creating activities and assignments that directly address these outcomes. Learning outcomes not only help students to know what is important but also remind us what is important.
- Learning outcomes help assess how well the learning strategies you are using are working or not working. Without clear and specific learning outcomes, it is difficult to say if you have been successful in teaching your course. Students may report they like the class, and they may do well on tests. But using your learning outcomes allows faculty to develop student assessment practices that reveal whether the classroom activities or assignments promoted the learning that we wanted for our students. If we find that we have not been as successful in helping students achieve the knowledge, skills, or behavior we were hoping for, we are able to review our practices. Maybe we actually need to be clearer about our desired learning outcomes, or maybe we need to think about another way to teach or to assess this outcome.

Again, in thinking about integrative learning, you can set specific integrative learning outcomes for your course, provide an ePortfolio assignment that facilitates the integration of your course's learning outcomes, or both. Next, we talk about establishing integrative learning outcomes, followed by a discussion of creating your ePortfolio assignment. Finally, we discuss using the process of backward design described by Wiggins and McTighe (2005) to help you begin to think about how to actually incorporate practices that encourage integrative learning in your classroom. Before we talk specifically about integrative learning outcomes, however, let's first review what we know about learning outcomes in general.

LEARNING OUTCOMES

In developing learning outcomes, the first place to start is with the following questions: What do I hope my students will learn in this class? How will they think and feel about the topic after they take the course? What will they be able to do as a result of taking this course? Learning outcomes, then, are statements that specify what learners will know or be able to do as a result of your course. Learning outcomes are usually expressed in terms of what one will know (knowledge), what one will think or feel (attitude), or what one will be able to do (skills) after completing a course. It is important to note that learning outcomes are focused on what the student does, not what the faculty member does. Learning outcomes aren't about what we cover as instructors in a course but what our students are able to know, think, and do after completing the course.

Well-written learning outcomes should be

- detailed and specific,
- measurable, and
- something that is done by the student and is a result of the learning experience in your course or program.

When writing learning outcomes, many faculty find Bloom's (1956) *Taxonomy of Educational Objectives*, revised by Anderson and Krathwohl (2001), particularly helpful. Because the taxonomy identifies increasing levels of cognitive skills, it can help faculty specify the level they hope their students will achieve.

The six levels of the taxonomy from lowest to highest cognitive skills are

1. knowledge/remembering
2. comprehension/understanding
3. application/applying
4. analysis/analyzing
5. synthesis/creating
6. evaluation/evaluating

Using Bloom's (1956) taxonomy can help you identify verbs to describe student learning. Here are some examples of learning outcome verbs:

- knowledge/remembering: *define, list, recognize*
- comprehension/understanding: *characterize, describe, explain, identify, locate, recognize, sort*
- application/applying: *choose, demonstrate, implement, perform*
- analysis/analyzing: *analyze, categorize, compare, differentiate*
- synthesis/creating: *construct, design, formulate, organize, synthesize*
- evaluation/evaluating: *assess, critique, evaluate, rank, rate*

Because learning outcomes are supposed to be detailed and specific, we suggest you avoid some verbs or terms, such as *understand, appreciate, know about, become familiar with, learn about,* and *become aware of.*

No doubt you have created learning outcomes for your courses already, and they might read like this:

- Students will analyze the relationship between the language of satire to literary form by the close examination of a selected number of 18th-century texts in a written essay.
- Students will be able to apply structured interview techniques in their fieldwork assignment.
- Students will be able to explain the economic and political factors that led to the start of the Iraq War.
- Students will develop an argument for a position on a controversial topic using literature to support their opinion.

Most faculty we talk with about developing integrative learning outcomes for their courses at first insist that they do it in their courses. Of course, we want our students to be able to integrate their learning, making connections between prior classes or their experiences at home and in the workplace, and we expect them to leave our class with this. Students often insist that this occurs in class discussions and in their final research papers. It may be true that there are other opportunities to integrate learning in their courses, but not all of your students will know and understand that this is something they should be focusing on. However, we remind you of the benefits of being explicit about your learning outcomes. Remember that part of the equation of integrative learning is intention. If we don't make the goal explicit, our students don't have the opportunity to make this learning intentional. If it is useful to develop learning outcomes for your course content, it is likely to be useful to develop learning outcomes for integrative learning too. As with content-focused learning outcomes, the best place to start is with questions such as the following: What do I want students to learn? What do I want students to think or feel? And what do I hope students will be able to do based on taking this course? Fortunately, the Association of American Colleges and Universities (AAC&U) (n.d.) VALUE rubric for integrative learning (see Chapter 2, pp. 29–30) can help us focus these learning outcomes too. The categories can help us develop specific integrative learning outcomes. Table 3.1 provides some examples of learning outcomes using the guidelines for creating well-written learning outcomes and the AAC&U (n.d.) categories for integrative learning.

As you can imagine, stating integrative learning outcomes explicitly will help you determine what you do in the classroom and will help students focus their attention in the right place. Defining learning outcomes is just the beginning. They provide the guidance necessary to help you determine what and how you work with your students. Once you have determined learning outcomes for your course, it is time

Table 3.1
Integrative Learning Outcomes Examples

Integrative Learning Category	Example Learning Outcomes
Connections to experience	• Students will apply two theories learned from the course to their community-based learning experience. • Students will demonstrate their understanding of Erikson's developmental theory by analyzing their developmental path in an autobiographical essay.
Connections to discipline	• Students will describe how a historian would analyze the problem identified in our community learning project.
Transfer	• Students will assess the knowledge from Psych 101 and develop a learning plan for this course based on this assessment.
Integrated communication	• In all written assignments, students will use appropriate communication strategies, including use of language and visual representations (as discussed in class).
Reflection and self-assessment	• Students will advance their writing skills by reflecting on what they have learned from each writing assignment.

to ask yourself how to use your time with your students and what assignments will assist them in demonstrating their achievement in these outcomes. We have found a model developed by Wiggins and McTighe (2005) called *backward design* to be helpful in conceptualizing what we need to do to incorporate integrative learning into our courses. Also, Dee Fink's (2003) *Creating Significant Learning Experiences* is a helpful process in rethinking one's syllabus in light of the development of learning outcomes. Of course, we think the ePortfolio is one of the assignments you should choose to help your students demonstrate achieving your learning outcomes.

BACKWARD DESIGN

According to Wiggins and McTighe (2005), the three steps of backward course design are identify desired results, determine acceptable evidence, and plan learning experiences and instruction. By writing clear and specific learning outcomes for your course overall, and possibly for integrative learning, you have already done the first step.

In determining acceptable evidence, Wiggins and McTighe (2005) are referring to assignments that facilitate the development of artifacts and allow students to demonstrate what you want your students to learn. Thinking through your course by focusing on what you'd like to see in the end provides a fresh look on how to approach your courses. It isn't just a matter of deciding which chapters of the text you cover and how many pages the final paper should have; the process helps you to really

Table 3.2
Integrative Learning Backward Design Example

Learning Outcome	Assignment	Activities to Support
Students will describe how a historian would analyze the problem identified in our community learning project.	Historical perspectives paper: 5 pages using historiography model	Reading, lectures, and discussions on historiography Smaller assignments: • Field notes • Community document reviews • Historiography quizzes Class discussions: documentation and connection to historical concepts
Students will assess the knowledge from Psych 101 and develop a learning plan for this course based on this assessment.	Learning plan paper	Psych 101 concept quiz Missing "data" worksheet: • Concepts I didn't know • Where I can find information Class discussion: need for transfer of information from Psych 101 to Psych 102

think about what you as faculty will need to do to facilitate students' learning what you want them to learn. As an example, in Table 3.2 let's take a few of the integrative learning outcomes we identified in Table 3.1 and use this model to think about how this translates in the classroom.

As you can see from these few examples, identifying the learning outcome is just the first step. For instance, if you want students to incorporate disciplinary concepts into their understanding of a problem, as in the first example, you will need to design an assignment that helps the student develop and demonstrate the learning outcome. In this case, the assignment is the historical perspectives paper. In addition, you need to consider what students need to experience to be able to successfully learn and demonstrate what you want them to learn. Giving background about the topic via lecture, reading, and discussion are standard ways we typically help students learn material. But smaller assignments that lead to the final project are equally important in helping students achieve our goals. In this case, learning to take field notes and gather data from the community organization's documents is necessary to be able to apply the practice of historiography in this course. And finally, discussions throughout the course about the process leading up to the final assignment can be helpful.

THE EPORTFOLIO IN YOUR CLASS OR PROGRAM

Of course, all the learning outcomes in your course are important, and the ePortfolio provides a way for students to demonstrate their competencies in all or some of them as well as provides a platform to make sense of how they all fit together.

The ePortfolio will likely be one of many assignments you give in a course or one that students complete at the end of their program. Typically, the ePortfolio is the culminating showcase assignment that allows students to learn and demonstrate their learning in all or most of the learning outcomes for the course. If a course learning outcome is related to writing abilities or critical thinking or applying a theoretical perspective, these competencies would probably show up in the ePortfolio and could be evaluated using the ePortfolio. Whether you explicitly state that integrative learning is a learning outcome in the course, the ePortfolio is where integration of one's learning can and often does occur. It provides a structure for the way all the learning outcomes in a course come together.

You could assign several types of ePortfolios in your course or program: working, project or task, and showcase. These assignments can stand on their own, but if you (or you and your colleagues who are working on a larger ePortfolio process for your students) choose, you could use all three of these ePortfolio assignments in your course or program.

A working ePortfolio assignment asks students to collect and reflect. Students are asked to collect all or much of their assignments in the course as well as reflect on their learning through directed reflection prompts. These artifacts can be housed in the working ePortfolio. Students can also be encouraged or directed to collect other artifacts, such as photos they have taken that relate to the course or their lives outside the course, links to relevant or important websites, and even work done outside your course or program. The goal of the working ePortfolio is to help students create a space where they can collect and reflect on a lot of artifacts and content. To create a showcase, students have to have something to select, so the collection and reflection part is a very important process.

Students can also be asked to create a project or task ePortfolio, which is focused on representing the process and product of a particular project assigned in a course or program. These can be individual or small-group ePortfolios. For example, instead of a traditional lab book assignment, students could be asked to create an ePortfolio to document the process of an experiment, including the process and the outcome. This kind of assignment asks students to document the multiple steps necessary for completing an assigned task; it also serves as a way to document the final product.

Most ePortfolio assignments are showcase ePortfolios, typically cumulative representations of a student's work in a course or program. They showcase the student's work and can be the finished product. These portfolios represent the select, reflect, and assess part of the ePortfolio process. In a showcase portfolio, students select their best work and invite feedback and conversation. While a showcase ePortfolio is often the culminating assignment in a course or program, it can also be created outside the curriculum. The graduation ePortfolio at Clemson University is an example of this. ePortfolios designed to advance one's identity formation, career, or lifelong learning are also examples of showcase ePortfolios that can be created outside the curriculum.

Figure 3.1
Types of ePortfolios

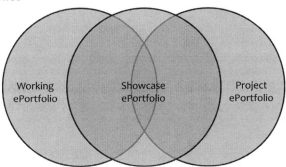

Figure 3.1 illustrates how these types of ePortfolios can function together. A student's working and project ePortfolios can become a part of his or her showcase ePortfolio.

THE EPORTFOLIO PROCESS

How we structure and support the development of any type of ePortfolio is important. That is really what this book is about—the pedagogical strategies that help students develop integrative learning ePortfolios. Some kind of ePortfolio assignment in your course or program is key. Guidelines and sample ePortfolio assignments are offered in Chapter 5. And one must include experiences that facilitate and lead up to an ePortfolio assignment. Many examples of assignments and the rationale behind them are presented in Chapters 4, 6, and 7. These are the activities and assignments in the backward design process that lead to the development of assignments, including the ePortfolio.

Whatever the activity, it is imperative to provide students with opportunities to become involved in the ePortfolio process. Early in the development of ePortfolios in education, administrators and faculty recognized that ePortfolios were more than just a technological tool. Helen Chen (Cambridge, Chen, & Ketcheson, 2004) coined the term *folio thinking,* which refers to the notion that an ePortfolio implies "a process of planning, keeping track of, making sense of, and sharing evidence of learning and performance." B. L. Cambridge (2001) lists three steps students can use in creating an ePortfolio—collect, select, and reflect—which serves as the foundation for facilitating the ePortfolio process or folio thinking in our courses or programs. Figure 3.2 illustrates an expanded conceptualization of the ePortfolio process that can be used in thinking about activities and assignments in our courses and programs.

Figure 3.2
The Integrative Learning ePortfolio Process

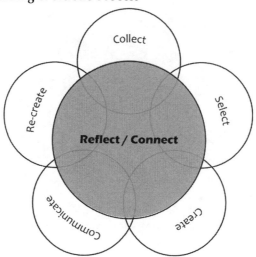

At the center of the process is reflection and connection. As we discuss in Chapter 2, integrative learning happens when we intentionally make connections across time and context. Reflection is the mechanism that allows us to make these connections. As reflection is in the center, activities and opportunities devoted to helping students make connections should be at the forefront of the activities you choose and develop in your course.

Collect refers to having students gather artifacts that could be used in their ePortfolios. In the context of a course, this means encouraging (or requiring) students to keep copies of their assignments, their work in the course, and other things that are related to their learning (photos, articles, links to relevant websites, and even ideas). Students are not typically in the habit of keeping their work or other artifacts related to their learning. Encouraging the practice of collecting one's work is important because without a reservoir of artifacts, it is difficult to reflect on and make connections with what a student has been learning. As described earlier, working ePortfolios involve students in the *collect* and *reflect* parts of the ePortfolio process, but obviously these are necessary for any kind of ePortfolio.

The *select* part of the process relates especially to the development of showcase ePortfolios as well as some forms of project ePortfolios. Depending on the purpose and audience of the ePortfolio, students can select artifacts that represent their best work, or in some cases they may choose work that shows a progression. As you can imagine, it is good practice to ask students to reflect on what they should select, what they select, and how and why it is important to their learning.

The *create* aspect of the ePortfolio process includes making the ePortfolio, using technology to build it, and making decisions about its architecture and structure.

While much of the design of an ePortfolio might be dictated by the assignment you give, much of any ePortfolio should be left for students to make their own, which of course involves reflection.

The *communicate* part of the ePortfolio process asks students to reflect on the purpose of the ePortfolio and consider their audience as they create it. After all, most ePortfolios are created for someone. In addition, an ePortfolio is not a one-way form of communication; it demands dialogue or feedback about the contents. This is evident when a student submits an ePortfolio assignment in a course and receives feedback from the instructor. But feedback can be given in many ways, including during small-group development of an ePortfolio and through peer review.

The conversation that ensues from the ePortfolio leads to the *re-create* part of the process, in which new thinking and revision or the impetus to create a new ePortfolio occurs, perhaps going from a working ePortfolio to a showcase ePortfolio.

Next we provide an example of a particular course and walk you through the process of integrating integrative learning and ePortfolios. Family studies is an interdisciplinary, term-long second-year general education course that is part of the University Studies program. ePortfolios have been used primarily in this yearlong first-year course but have begun to be used in sophomore-level courses too. As this is a term-long course (only 10 weeks), we use this as an example of how an ePortfolio can be incorporated in a short period. Some of the students in this class will have taken the first-year course, but many will have transferred into Portland State University with little or no experience in creating an ePortfolio. However, some created an ePortfolio in their Freshman Inquiry course, and in this case, the instructor encourages them to build their portfolio on their previous one.

Sonja Taylor, an instructor for this course, decided she wanted her students to be able to reflect on what they had learned in the course and connect it to their lived experience. "After all, we all have families and our own experience is part of our knowledge and attitudes about family. Understanding this and placing this knowledge in the context of the course is important. In fact, I don't think you can thoroughly understand the content without integrating your own knowledge of family" (S. Taylor, personal communication, June 28, 2013). Taylor also wants to encourage the development of metareflection, helping students understand what they have learned and how.

Taylor's stated learning outcomes have been developed by others in her department and are used across all sections of this course. They are in line with the University Studies program's general education goals:

- Critical Thinking: Analyze the historical, social, cultural, and economic context of family groups through application of relevant theories and conceptual frameworks.
- Communication: Increase awareness and communicate with other students and faculty to understand diversity of family, socially constructed views of family and the impact of assets and risks at the family, community and societal levels.

- Diversity of Human Experience: Increase knowledge of the complexity of individual and family development and the impact of culture, the economy, and public policies on historically marginalized family groups.
- Social and Ethical Responsibility: Increase understanding of individual and collective responsibility through examination of disparities in social success of individuals and families based upon societal oppression and privilege, and the responsibility of social structures to sustain diverse family groups. (S. Taylor, personal communication, June 28, 2013)

These learning outcomes don't completely follow the experts' suggestions for developing learning outcomes, which are a bit vague and may not be easily measurable. However, you can certainly see from these outcomes that students will have an idea of what they will learn in the course. In addition, this instructor had several integrative learning outcomes. For simplicity, in Table 3.3 we map one of the content-related outcomes and the instructor's integrative learning outcomes as we think about the backward design for this course.

Table 3.3
Family Studies Backward Design Example

Learning Outcome	Assignment	Activities to Support
Course content: Increase knowledge of the complexity of individual and family development and the impact of culture, the economy, and public policies on historically marginalized family groups.	• Final paper on issue affecting families (e.g., same-sex parents) using at least 2 theories from class • Final paper PowerPoint • ePortfolio	• Class readings • Class discussions • In-class activities • Final paper PowerPoint • Class readings • Class discussions • Final paper • Final PowerPoint • ePortfolio instructions
Integrative learning: Students will analyze their own family as a way to articulate and demonstrate understanding of the multiple-faceted ways of defining *family*.	• Family collage in ePortfolio	• Class readings • Class discussions • In-class activity • ePortfolio instructions
Integrative learning: Analyze and articulate what has been learned in the course about the content and about the learning process.	• Letter to future students in ePortfolio	• Class discussions • Course journals • ePortfolio instructions

Note in the content-related learning outcomes that students are being asked to connect their understanding of *family* to a variety of perspectives: economic, cultural, and public policy. This is an attempt to add integrative learning with this particular learning outcome as part of addressing the *diversity of human experience* learning outcome for the course. In addition, this instructor explicitly prioritizes integrative learning in the course through an emphasis on students' making connections with their own family backgrounds and by asking them to make metacognitive connections. Also, note that the final paper and final PowerPoint presentation for the class are not only assignments on their own but also activities that support the ePortfolio assignment. And the final paper PowerPoint presentation is an activity that supports the final paper.

The ePortfolio assignment for this course is, as you would expect, a showcase portfolio, demonstrating what students have learned in the course. But the ePortfolio for this class also incorporates a type of project ePortfolio, asking students to display the major projects for the course in the ePortfolio. These projects are sequential, and Taylor describes them like this:

> The collage provides [a] visual image and lets them think of family in a different way. The PowerPoint becomes their final paper. They get immediate feedback from me and use it for the final paper. With both posted on the portfolio, the students and I can see the evolution of their thought process. (S. Taylor, personal communication, June 28, 2013)

For those who have created an ePortfolio in earlier courses, this assignment invites them to integrate their learning into this course. Their previous ePortfolios serve as working portfolios and contribute to their current ePortfolio. This also encourages them to see the current ePortfolio as a working portfolio that can be adapted to their next ePortfolio. Figure 3.3 is one example of an ePortfolio submitted in this class.

Figure 3.3
Sample ePortfolio for Family Studies Course

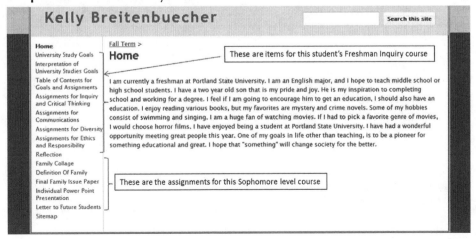

BALANCING CONTENT AND INTEGRATIVE LEARNING
GOALS AND OUTCOMES

Many in the academy argue that the goal in our academic courses is to impart knowl-edge. Thus, the content-related learning outcomes are the most important and should require the most attention. We certainly don't argue that content learning is important, whether in an English course or in resident assistant training—students need to be taught and learn the content to be able to perform well. However, as learn-ing theory and research (as we've discussed in earlier chapters and more in upcoming chapters) tells us, we need context to be able to fully and deeply understand a concept and be able to apply it. For example, in the family studies course described earlier, students can certainly learn the textbook definition of *family* and will likely be able to reliably state that definition on a test or in a paper. However, when we ask our students to make the connection between the textbook definition and their own fam-ily, they have the opportunity to understand fully the magnitude of that definition and to even analyze and critique the research-derived definition. Does this definition make sense with their own experience? The context of one's own family allows one to fully take in the concept of family. Of course, many students may be able to get to this deep level of connection without explicitly addressing it in the course. But many will not, and they will leave having memorized a definition for a single test but without an understanding of the rich and nuanced concept of family that they will continue to develop and understand the rest of their lives.

To us it sometimes seems like a false dichotomy when faculty or staff say they don't have time to create opportunities for integrative learning in their classrooms. If the goal of the course is to have students learn about a field, then we need to acknowl-edge that this learning does not and cannot happen in a vacuum. Without providing opportunities for students to integrate their learning with their previous experiences, previous courses, an understanding of their learning process, and so forth, we cannot expect them to learn the content of our courses as fully as we want them to. Making time to help students integrate their learning is important. Part Two provides some thoughts on classroom strategies that will help you do this.

PART TWO

Teaching for Integrative Learning

This section discusses promoting integrative learning in your class or program and focuses on four areas that we consider the foundation of ePortfolio practices:

1. reflection
2. making connections
3. lifelong learning
4. communication

Promoting these practices with our students happens in the creation of an ePortfolio but must be practiced and developed outside the ePortfolio too. There are guidelines and suggestions for activities that can be used in your classroom or program with or without an ePortfolio assignment. The activities discussed in these chapters, which are labeled "Activity suggestion," are by no means the only viable or even best activities but instead should be seen as idea generators for developing your own best practices.

Chapters 4 and 5 focus on classroom practices that can be considered scaffolding activities for an ePortfolio. Without practice in reflection and making connections, developing an integrative learning ePortfolio would be impossible. These ideas and activities can lead to the development of an integrative learning ePortfolio.

Chapters 6 and 7 focus on ideas and activities for development of the ePortfolio. Strategies for engaging students in the ePortfolio process can help them see the ePortfolio as a lifelong practice. As ePortfolios use multiple communication modalities, it is also important for students to participate in activities that help them think through their communication choices.

The chapters in this section answer the following questions:

Chapter 4: What is reflection? Why is it important for integrative learning? What are the guidelines in asking students to reflect? What are some specific activities for students that promote good reflective practice?

Chapter 5: Why is it important for students to make connections in a course or a program? What are some specific activities that promote helping students make connections? What does an ePortfolio assignment look like?

Chapter 6: Why should we promote lifelong learning? What should we consider to promote developing and valuing lifelong learning in students? What are some specific activities that promote lifelong learning using the ePortfolio?

Chapter 7: What does an ePortfolio communicate? Who is the audience? What is important to consider in helping students develop a digital identity through the ePortfolio? What are some specific activities that promote good communication practices?

As shown in Figure Part 2.1, this section addresses the foundational practices for helping students create an integrative learning ePortfolio.

Figure Part 2.1
Framework for Part Two

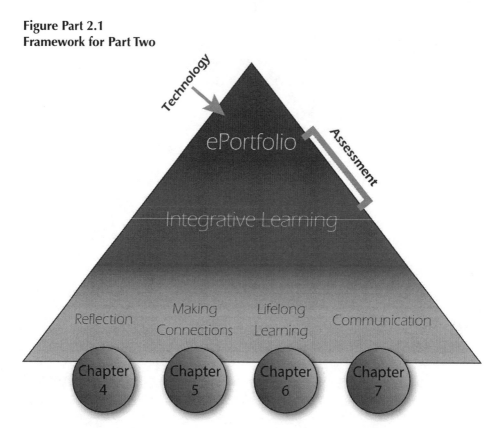

Chapter 4

Fostering Reflective Practice

Candyce's story: Reflection seems to come naturally to some of us. If someone asks me how I feel about something, I usually find it easy to pause, think, and quickly determine what I think and feel about whatever I've been asked, and even provide reasons why I think and feel that way. It is a rude awakening when I discover that my students do not seem to have that reflection gene. It troubles me so much that I have spent a lot of time thinking and writing about it in my teaching journal, which I try to write in after every class I teach. Looking back at some of my journal entries, I came across this one that illustrates the power of reflection and that reflection is a skill we learn, not one that necessarily comes easily.

So tonight, I asked students to get in small groups to talk about their reaction to our text using their reading reflection journals as their guides. Walking around and listening in, I ended up focusing on the group with Jason [name changed] and I was surprised to see him in a lively discussion and even more surprised to hear that he was admiring and asking Carla about her responses in her journal. How did she take notes? What did she do to come up with her responses? He seemed really impressed with what she had gotten out of the book and wanted to know how she did that. Note: I wonder if this will have an impact on Jason's future reflection journals—check on this. And time for me to think more about how I prep them for these reflection journals. I think I have something to learn from Carla. I wish I could have eavesdropped more.

We all agree that we want our students to practice reflection. No doubt, your syllabi have at least one reflective assignment. We tell our students over and over that reflection is an important part of the learning process, and it is touted as the centerpiece of ePortfolios. Without reflections, ePortfolios are just glorified file cabinets—a catalog of work with a brief index.

Russell Rogers (2001) and Carol Rogers (2002) point to the paradox in education, which is that we value and seem to understand the centrality of reflection in education, but we really don't seem to have an agreement about what it is and how to facilitate the process in our students. Varying conceptions of reflection make it difficult to think about how to approach teaching reflection in the classroom and its use in the ePortfolio. The entry for *reflection* in a thesaurus illustrates our difficulty. The suggested terms are as varied as *careful thought, assessment, consideration, soul searching, reasoning, introspection, focus,* and *forethought.*

And while educators are not agreed on one definition of *reflection,* they would likely agree when a good reflective essay crosses their desk. We often hear our colleagues lament the lack of thinking and insight in students' reflective work and speak effusively on the depth and inspiration in others, such as in the following:

> This is my final composition research paper. . . . I learned how to write a topic proposal [and] critical analysis along with other writing styles. I learned how to correctly write thesis statements, unified . . . paragraphs, and a memo format. Paraphrasing, in-text citations, MLA documentation, and transitions were commonplace and necessary for a quality paper. I learned how to organize materials . . . [and how to] utilize the library databases. (Jenson, 2011, p. 50)

Compare it to this example:

> I have learned how to ask some [of] those "wh" questions. Why? Who said? I want proof, and if there is truth to something, then that shouldn't be a problem! In the real world I need to be able to think for myself, so learning to be critical is very important. (Jenson, 2011, p. 57)

While the student in the first example undoubtedly answered the prompt from the professor, the essay lacks insight and adds little to the discussion of the student's work. The second reflection, however, also responds to the faculty prompt but in a way that exemplifies why we think reflection is such a good idea in education. It provides evidence of the student struggling with an issue and making connections that might have been unlikely without a reflective activity. The second example is more demonstrative of what we hope to see when we assign reflective activities.

This chapter discusses current thought on reflection and its role in integrative learning and in ePortfolios and presents ideas on how to teach students to be reflective practitioners. It provides ideas for reflection prompts and assignments.

WHAT IS REFLECTION?

Merriam-Webster's defines *reflection* (n.d.) as "a thought, idea, or opinion formed or a remark made as a result of meditation" and "consideration of some subject matter, idea, or purpose." It sounds easy enough, but it is far more complicated. If you look at all the articles and books about reflection, you would think it is a well-understood concept in education, but it is actually far from it. Authors have written about reflection as a cognitive activity (e.g., Loughran, 1996), an affective process (e.g., Boud, Keogh, & Walker, 1985), as necessitating an examination of one's beliefs

---

Exhibit 4.1
Guiding Principles of Reflection

1. Reflection is a meaning-making process that moves a learner from one experience into the next with deeper understanding of its relationships with and connections to other experiences and ideas. It is the thread that makes continuity of learning possible, and ensures the progress of the individual.
2. Reflection is a systematic, rigorous, disciplined way of thinking.
3. Reflection needs to happen in community, in interaction with others.
4. Reflection requires attitudes that value the personal and intellectual growth of oneself and of others.

Note. From "Defining Reflection: Another Look at John Dewey and Reflective Thinking," by C. Rogers, 2002, *Teachers College Record, 104*(4), 845. Copyright 2002 by Teachers College, Columbia University.

(e.g., Dewey, 1933), and even as a process that requires substantial change in one's thinking (e.g., Mezirow, 1991). One, some, or all of them would be correct depending on the purpose of the reflective activity. The reality is that there is no one right way to reflect, and in fact it depends on what you want your students to learn by participating in reflection. We believe that having a good conceptual framework to guide your classroom practice can help you determine what you want your students to learn from reflective activities and guide the development of classroom practices and course assignments. Carol Rogers (2002) developed a framework for teachers for thinking about reflection that has been helpful to us in creating environments and activities that promote the kind of reflection we would like to see in students (see Exhibit 4.1). These principles are derived from her synthesis of Dewey's (1933, 1938, 1944) ideas about reflection. The following is a discussion about these guiding principles.

Reflection as a Meaning-Making Process

In this first principle the word *experience* is crucial, and Dewey's (1938) ideas about experience are helpful in thinking about how we create opportunities for students to make meaning in their reflective activities in the classroom and in their ePortfolios. To Dewey, experience is more than just participation. Experience is about interaction and continuity. First, experience necessities some kind of interaction with one's environment. This interaction can manifest itself in many ways, for example, between the student and other students or the professor, between oneself and the natural environment, or between a student and the ideas presented in a text. The environment can be anything the student interacts with. In interacting with the environment, Dewey (1933, 1938) suggests that students fundamentally change as part of this interaction, that they see and understand things differently. Carol Rogers (2002) also highlights Dewey's (1938) concept of continuity in the context of meaning making. A student's experience does not happen out of context. How we make meaning depends on our past experiences and prior knowledge. Dewey also talks about continuity more broadly. Continuity adds to the collective understanding and creation of knowledge; we advance our knowledge base and our social connections through this continuity. In other words, we learn from our experiences through making connections. Simply stated, the equation is

interaction + continuity = experience

According to Carol Rogers (2002), "Without interaction learning is sterile and passive, never fundamentally changing the learner. Without continuity, learning is random and disconnected, building toward nothing either within the learner or in the world" (p. 847).

The first example of a reflection on p. 56 demonstrates that the student participated in the activity but essentially did not discuss how she interacted with this assignment or the ways her participation in the activity was *connected* to anything larger than that single event. It is likely that this student did make connections between her participation and something else. It might have occurred to her fleetingly that she learned something she could apply in the future to her other classes, if not beyond. She might have had an aha moment about how systems such as library databases are organized similarly to the data management system she uses at her job or is learning about in her computer science classes. In the second reflection example, the student interacted with the material in a way that allowed her to make connections between her participation and the larger concept of evidence and showed her how she can use the skill of critically examining ideas in the future. We see our jobs as instructors to facilitate reflective processes that invite students to make these kinds of connections. In providing opportunities to make connections, our students can have an *experience* rather than just participate in an activity. This is not to say that students will not make these connections without our intervention; some will, but with guidance many more are likely to make those connections.

We are not suggesting what a student should be making connections to. Some authors argue that true reflection entails specific step-by-step processes to be able to be called "reflection" (e.g., Ash & Clayton, 2009; Gibbs, 1988; C. Rogers, 2002). Others argue that reflective activities should be geared toward creating disequilibrium in one's thinking, requiring students to fundamentally question their beliefs (e.g., Brookfield, 1990; Mezirow, 1990). Our suggestion is much simpler: Invite students to make connections between what they are learning in your course and something else. You decide. The point is that we need to create opportunities for students to actively engage (interact) with what they are learning as well as help them connect (create continuity) with what they already know or is already known. Part of the difficulty in using reflective processes in teaching and for assignments is that there are no right answers to a reflective prompt. Each student's interaction and connection to his or her knowledge base and experience will be different. As Aldous Huxley (1933) said, "Experience is not what happens to you; it's what you do with what happens to you" (p. 5).

Reflection as a Way of Thinking

According to Carol Rogers (2002), "Reflection is a systematic, rigorous, disciplined way of thinking" (p. 845). Rogers describes the process of reflection as following the lines of inquiry in the scientific method, including naming a problem that derives from one's experience to hypothesizing about the experience to making decisions about the experience based on the testing of hypotheses. While this is definitely a reasonable and logical way to teach and ask students to engage in reflection, it does not need to be as detailed to result in meaningful reflection. In fact, we propose that imposing this high-level standard may actually cause the reflective practice that we ask of students to be just an academic hoop to jump through and not a habit of mind that they can use consistently in their day-to-day lives. We agree that reflection needs to be systematic and rigorous but argue that depending on the complexity and importance of the task it might be a relatively simple process that doesn't require a step-by-step detailed analysis of an experience.

In writing about reflection, Dewey (1933, 1938) contrasts it to stream of consciousness and beliefs. All too often, our students (and their instructors sometimes) mistake this kind of thinking for reflection. A student writes about what happened in a class project team meeting with excruciating detail but with little description or analysis or understanding of what happened (stream of consciousness); another student writes about a reading on poverty and discusses the "welfare cheats" in the student's neighborhood without incorporating any new perspective offered in the reading or in discussions with classmates (beliefs). The process of reflection that we use in our classrooms and encourage through the use of ePortfolios needs to be systematic, rigorous, and disciplined. Because of this, developing good reflective prompts is important. Depending on what you are hoping students will learn, these prompts will be more or less detailed but nonetheless ask students to be systematic, rigorous, and disciplined.

Reflection and Learning as a Social Activity

"Reflection needs to happen in community, in interaction with others" (C. Rogers, 2002, p. 845). When reflection and community are mentioned in the same sentence, instructors and staff often get a confused look on their faces. Isn't reflection by its nature an individual activity? Wouldn't sharing or working together on reflective activities actually encourage students to steal others' ideas? If you think about another definition of *reflection*, such as one's reflection seen in water, it makes sense that reflection is social by nature. Reflection involves some kind of feedback, and without that feedback, we don't have a sense of what we are looking at and trying to understand. When we look in the water, we see a reflection of our face, not a true representation of what is but a different view or perspective. Reflection as a learning tool is like this too. The feedback we get from sharing our reflections or creating our reflections with others parallels this phenomenon. It is only when we share our thoughts and feelings with others that we get a true sense of our ideas. Rogers points out three benefits of collaborative reflection:

1. Sharing reflections helps one see the importance of an experience. Without sharing one's ideas with others, one might dismiss his or her ideas as irrelevant or unimportant.
2. By sharing one's ideas with others, one has the opportunity to see the phenomenon in a new light. A fellow student might see the issue differently, providing a different perspective.
3. Sharing one's reflection provides support for the process of reflection, illustrates the importance of taking time to reflect, and provides a space for it to happen. It is often too easy to just take in information without reflection. Sharing with others provides an opportunity to make time to reflect.

This does not mean that reflection is always, nor should it always be, a public endeavor, which would be absurd in a classroom setting. There wouldn't be enough time for students to share everything you wanted them to reflect on. Also, some reflections should be kept private for quiet contemplation. In thinking about this principle, consider activities that incorporate sharing ideas. An activity can be informal, such as turning to a neighbor to share thoughts about a quote in a text, or it can be more formal, such as a peer review of a paper or a public critique of an ePortfolio.

Reflection as Attitudes

"Reflection requires attitudes that value the personal and intellectual growth of oneself and of others" (C. Rogers, 2002, p. 845). In higher education we can sometimes forget that as human beings we are not merely brains; we also have emotions. Dewey (1933, 1938) was aware that we overlook the affective side of our learners at our peril and at theirs. If we ignore that our students come to our classes with feelings and opinions that shape their understanding, we miss the opportunity to engage our students' affect in a positive way. Rogers (2002) says Dewey "recognized the tendency in all human beings to see what we wish were true, or what we fear is true, rather than to accept what evidence tells us is so" (p. 858), which teaches students how to approach reflection with an attitude of wholeheartedness and open-mindedness. Rogers (2002) suggests that these attitudes, among others, such as responsibility, directedness, and readiness, are essential for true reflection and that we should foster them in our students. Attitudes are not easily taught, but how we approach our work with our students and how we value what we ask them to do can make a difference in how they approach the work of learning.

Wholeheartedness is the enthusiasm we bring to an endeavor. Reflection without active engagement can simply be an assignment one has to complete. Wholehearted-ness is bound to rub off on others. Our excitement about a topic or even the process of reflection can influence students' approach to their assignments.

Open-mindedness refers to the ability to recognize our own perspective and invite that of others. We tend to fall back on comfortable ways of thinking and feeling. The reality is that learning is sometimes frightening. It can mean giving up well-loved ideas and being left with little or no understanding of the world around us. Being open-minded is actually a brave act. It means we are willing to take a risk and let go of the known to discover a new truth. Open-mindedness can also refer to allowing one to be playful with ideas and imagination. As faculty, we don't often encourage this kind of playfulness because we usually know what direction we would like to see our students take. Open-mindedness applies to faculty as well as students, and you must be open to how students share what they learn.

In higher education, we talk about the role of a liberal education as fostering lifelong learning and developing enduring habits of mind. The process of reflection is one way we can help students develop the habits of mind we hope our students leave our classes with. Without students learning and developing the skills of reflection, these attitudes may not develop as fully as we'd like. In fact, if our students gain nothing else, we hope they gain the ability to reflect.

These principles are all good and well, inspiring and aspirational, but you are probably wondering what it is like to use them in practice. The next section describes in detail reflective activities and reflection assignments that you can use as is or that you can adapt to your course or program.

IDEAS FOR APPLYING THESE PRINCIPLES

The activities in this section can be used to help students develop ePortfolios, but they can be used in any classroom. The trick to helping students develop a reflective practice and ultimately demonstrate high levels of insight is just that—practice. You will notice that many of these activities don't seem related to ePortfolio reflections, but we have found them to be useful in helping students develop the practice of reflection.

The suggested activities in this chapter are organized into the following categories:

- Set the tone: Reflection is learning.
- It's the little things that count.
- Know your goal: Reflect on what matters.
- Consider various forms of reflection.
- Make it more complicated.
- Learning is social: Make reflection a conversation.

After introducing these categories, we list several suggestions for activities you can use or adapt.

Set the Tone: Reflection Is Learning

If you want your students to become reflective practitioners, you need to provide them with opportunities to understand the connection of reflection to their learning, harness their innate ability to reflect and use it in a variety of ways and contexts, and model or show good reflective practice.

Activity suggestion: Opening letters. One way we have found to set the tone and provide an early opportunity to engage in reflection and model reflective practice is a welcome letter to students, in which the instructor introduces himself or herself to the students, shares the particular goals for the course, and engages students in a dialogue about their hopes and fears for the course. In many of my, Candyce's, courses, this is the first writing assignment, and it counts for points in the course. In the past, I would always have some kind of making-connections and goal-setting activity at the beginning of class. I would have a discussion about the reasons students were taking the class, I would have an assignment that asked them to set goals for their learning in the class, and I would ask them how this particular class fits into their academic pursuits and what they hope to get out of it. Most of these activities fell short of what I expected. Students certainly responded to the prompts I gave them (especially if there were points involved), but the responses were often lackluster or pro forma. I realized over time that I was asking them to do something out of context, thus making the activity seem relevant only in the confines of the course. What I really wanted to do was begin a relationship with them and invite them on the journey (albeit brief) of learning together. My assignments attempted to do this but were really one-sided. While I certainly talked about my intentions for the assignments in class and even had the rationale on the prompt, I was essentially asking them to reflect without my having to show them that I was engaged in the process too. The letter I write to my classes serves as a way to model reflective practice as they see my thought processes and my biases in a more personal and transparent way. The letter creates the expectation that reflection will be an important part of their learning. And finally, the letter invites them to take the time to share their thoughts, connecting personally with me in an academic setting. This assignment has changed the tone of my courses. My students get to know a little about me and I get to know my students at the beginning (I even get an early sense of their ability to write). And it tells them that there will be more than learning content in the course; I expect them to engage in and reflect on their own learning process as well as what they are learning in the course.

This assignment could be incorporated as a blog post, by e-mail, or even as part of a discussion thread in an online course. I have found, though, that students in this era find the idea of a physical letter quaint and are intrigued by the notion of doing something that many of them have never done. I prefer for them to type the letter but invite them to handwrite it if they want to (and many of them do). Some actually bring me a letter written on stationery complete with matching envelope. If I am not using this assignment in a fully online class, I ask them to bring the letter to class with them. I give them my letter on the first day and expect their response at the next class meeting. I always answer their response letters with notes that are usually quite brief and for the most part encouraging. It is a great opportunity to make connections between what students are hoping to get in the class and what my plans are for the course. It also provides me a way to push those who completed the assignment in a halfhearted way with encouragement and a low score.

In my Freshman Inquiry class, I started with a two-page, single-spaced letter that opened with why I was writing to them: "I am writing to orient you to me and to the class. I want to know you and I want you to know me." I shared some personal information on my family status, educational background including the fact that I'm a first-generation college student, and a little about my career path that led to me being their instructor. The majority of the letter describes my orientation to the class and my expectations of myself and of them, as the following excerpt shows:

> I want to assure you that most of what we do in this class has a purpose and is based upon a body of research that suggests that the activity is useful for student learning. In other words, when you think that something we are doing is hokey, boring, etc., think about what the purpose of the activity might be. Ask about it! In this class, you will not only be learning about the topic of work and play, but also about the process of learning. If you don't get it, you aren't learning. Last, I want to acknowledge what a time of transition this is for all of us.

I am always surprised by the willingness of students to converse with me through these letters. The vehicle of letter writing and the modeling I do in reflecting about myself and my own ideas about teaching seem to help them reflect on themselves and their role as learners. The following are excerpts from students' letters:

> It is a relief to know that no one in your family went to college. It gives me hope that I can do well. I feel like I am my family's hope. I feel good knowing that you might understand this and that I can ask you for help along the way. Being the first in my family to go to college might not be a bad thing after all.

I have always hated the classes where the teacher makes you talk with other students. The teacher's job is to teach. The students' job is to listen. I realized after reading your letter that maybe I just didn't understand what the teacher was trying to do. I can't promise to be excited about talking with other students because old habits are hard to break but I will try to remember what you said about everything we are doing is done for a reason.

I have always been a do it the last minute kind of gal. I realize that maybe this won't work in the class and maybe not in other college classes either. I don't know how to change this but I think I better try.

It's the Little Things That Count

Setting the tone doesn't mean doing one activity in the beginning of a class and then checking that off your list of things to do. To help students develop practices and put reflection at the forefront, you must continue to provide ways for them to engage in reflective practice. Here are some really quick and easy activities that will help students learn about and practice reflection.

- Point out reflection when you see it: As humans, we reflect constantly but don't always recognize that is what we are doing or how or why it is important. Naming and acknowledging this natural phenomenon can help students more consciously engage in the process.
  - *Activity suggestion: Look for reflection in student discussions.* Comment on them. Point out what they are doing well in this regard. Student: "I kind of see the author's point. It is like the text we were talking about earlier." You: "Yes, I can see the connection you are making. I can see you took the time to make connections between what might have looked disparate. Good job reflecting on that. Now let's talk about that idea."
  - *Activity suggestion: Share your reflections with students and name them.* "In rereading the text for today's class, I was struck by the connection between these ideas and what happened on my morning commute."
  - *Activity suggestion: Point out examples of reflection in the texts you are reading and in movies or film clips you use in the class.* Again, reflection is all around us. We just need to look for it and point it out.
- Use classroom assessment techniques (CATs) to give students quick opportunities to reflect. Although these ideas described in Angelo and Cross's 1993 book were intended to be a way for faculty to improve their practice through quick formative assessment of student learning, they are also a way for students to engage in their learning. These are typically very short activities that can be a routine part of the class. Many of our colleagues complete a CAT at every class session. The following are CATs you can use to encourage students in

reflecting on the content of the course and their own learning process. It is helpful to return these short assignments to your students so they can use them to watch the development of their ideas throughout the term.

- *Activity suggestion: Use minute papers.* Ask students to answer the question, What was the most important thing you learned during this class? or What important question remains unanswered? in the last 5 minutes of class. Any question that triggers students to reflect on something from the class can be asked. Students must reflect and self-assess to answer the question. Instructors collect written feedback on student learning, reflect on what they have learned from the minute papers, and address any issues at the beginning of the next class.

- *Activity suggestion: Background knowledge probe.* Ask students to answer two or three open-ended questions that probe the students' existing knowledge of a concept, subject, or topic. This is useful as a prior learning assessment to get an idea about what students know, but it is also an opportunity for students to take time to think about and reflect on what they already know about a topic. You can also ask students follow-up questions based on their responses to these questions later in the course, such as, What knowledge that you identified earlier have you used so far in the class? How do these topics relate?

- *Activity suggestion: Documented problem solutions.* Ask students to solve two or three problems and briefly explain each step in writing; students learn to reflect on the steps they took to solve the problem. The explanation of the steps (the process) is the purpose of the activity, not the actual solution (the product).

- *Activity suggestion: Directed paraphrasing.* Ask students to paraphrase a part of a lesson for a specific audience and purpose using their own words; students develop the skill of translating information into other words in other contexts. Doing this is a great activity to help them get experience in understanding different audiences, but expressing what they have learned in different ways also helps them learn and retain the information better.

- *Activity suggestion: Approximate analogies.* Ask students to complete the second part of an analogy in a few minutes, for example, Writing is to critical thinking as horseshoes are to horses. This activity helps students see what they are learning in a different light and connects what they are learning with things they already know. This is a great activity to help students begin to see patterns in what they are learning.

- *Activity suggestion: Application cards.* Ask students to write down one possible real-world application of what they have just learned; students connect newly learned concepts with prior knowledge and see the relevance of what they are learning.

Know Your Goal: Reflect on What Matters

As we said earlier, there really is no right way to reflect. However, for students to benefit from the process of reflecting, we need to be clear about what we want them to do and why. Although we believe we should follow the principles of reflection discussed earlier, the focus of reflective activities can be very different depending on your goals for the course or program. For example, for certain topics, you may want students to focus on a more cognitive task, reflecting on making connections between concepts they learned in a prerequisite course and the ideas in the syllabus. Or in a service-learning course, you might want students to take a more affective stance and ask them to reflect and write or even draw something representing their reactions to the first visit at their service site. Here are some ideas to consider as you set goals for reflection activities in your classroom.

Write effective prompts. It is easy to assume that students can read and follow instructions, but it is often the case that our students are not able to read between the lines and really understand our expectations when we ask them to reflect. Getting students to engage in reflective activities is difficult. It requires the faculty member to think (reflect) and develop thoughtful prompts, motivate and reward students for engaging in the activity, and give students the time necessary to make reflection occur. Students have to see it as a valuable activity (either intrinsically or extrinsically or both) and commit the time and mind power to make it happen. The first step is letting them know explicitly what you expect.

Base reflection on timing. Most of us think of reflection as happening after an event. However, reflection prompts can be directed retrospectively but also in anticipation of or even during an event.

Activity suggestion: Anticipatory reflection. These reflective prompts ask students to reflect on what they might expect from an activity or event. The opening letter activity described earlier in this chapter is an example of anticipatory reflection. It asks students to think about what they will bring to the course, what they hope to learn, and what goals they would like to pursue. It could be a reflection about how they want to approach writing a particular paper assignment: what has worked in the past, what they would like to take forward, and what they might want to experiment with as they approach this assignment. Carol Gabrielli, an instructor in a service-learning senior capstone course at Portland State University (PSU), took students through a guided imagery exercise before their first meeting at a community organization. She asked them to visualize what they would see and experience, and, most important, how they wanted to act and the impression they wanted to make on their new colleagues. How did they want to approach the encounter? She then asked them to imagine how they want to feel when they finish the course and then imagine themselves looking back over the experience and seeing what they have done to accomplish that outcome.

Activity suggestion: During an event. This type of reflection is often referred to as "reflection in action." While this kind of reflection is often difficult to facilitate, it can sometimes provide some of the best opportunities students have to learn how to reflect and take action in the moment. This type of reflection has been encouraged for professional development for people such as physicians, who must be able to reflect on what is happening and make a decision often in a life-or-death situation (see Schön, 1983). While being able to reflect in the moment may not necessarily save a life, it can help students learn about themselves in a particular context and help them make decisions in the moment or in the future.

The following is a reflection-in-action activity to encourage students to look at their behavior in a group and consider what they could do to move the group process forward. In preparing for a large group project, Candyce asks students to read an article on group roles and tasks (transactional and procedural) and discuss it in class. She then asks students who are already in assigned groups to begin to work together in class on their group projects. Every 15 minutes, she tells them to stop, reflect, and quickly write about their role in the group at that moment, the tasks they were completing, and what they could do to make the work flow better.

Activity suggestion: After an event. Every assignment is an opportunity for reflection and to help students make connections. For example, with every paper they submit, you can ask students for a short paragraph reflecting on what they learned in writing the paper. You can ask them how they incorporated remarks you made on their last paper into this paper. You could also ask them to write about how this assignment related to another assignment in your class or even to something they have learned elsewhere. After students receive grades on a multiple-choice test, you can ask them to reflect on areas they did well on and areas they were weaker on and to analyze how they prepared for the test. The reflection could help them prepare for future tests.

In many instances, structured reflection prompts that are repeated over time can be useful in helping students develop reflective practice in analyzing situations and their actions. Gibbs (1988) provides a popular structured format that can be used to help understand a critical incident of any kind. In this model of reflection, students are instructed to go through a series of questions to analyze a situation. They first start with a clear description of what happened without using subjective adjectives or adverbs. They discuss their feelings about the situation, evaluate what was good or bad about it, and then begin to think or write about how to make sense of the situation. They can then reflect on what else they could have done. Finally, they can develop an action plan based on their complete analysis of the situation.

The DEAL model is a three-step reflection process that asks students to describe, examine, and articulate learning (Ash & Clayton, 2009). This model was developed especially for service-learning activities, but a version could be used for reflection after almost any event. Like the Gibbs (1988) model, the DEAL model starts with asking students to describe objectively what they are seeing as they engage in service and seek to apply the learning in their service setting. The model then directs students to examine what they see through three types of prompts: personal growth (e.g., What strengths and weaknesses emerge?), social responsibility (e.g., What are we trying to accomplish?), and course content (e.g., What academic content applies?). After this, students are asked to step back and describe what and how they learned from the experience.

Consider Various Forms of Reflection

While reflection is typically seen as a writing task, reflection can also involve artistic expressions, such as drawings, sculpture, or dance. It can also involve using organizational representations such as a matrix to categorize ideas; a mind map to represent how a student sees concepts fitting together; or the creation of a Venn diagram, which helps students conceptualize overlapping concepts. The following activities are examples of these ideas.

Activity suggestion: Defining features matrix. Ask students to check off features in a table that distinguish between two or three similar concepts (see Tables 4.1 and 4.2).

Exhibit 4.2 shows a variation on the defining features matrix that is used to help students in the Postsecondary, Adult, and Continuing Education program at PSU begin to build a showcase ePortfolio to demonstrate their learning of program-defined learning outcomes. Students start by brainstorming what they have learned

Table 4.1
Defining Features Matrix Example 1

Features	Mammals	Reptiles
Fur	X	
Cold-blooded		X
Have hearts	X	X

Table 4.2
Defining Features Matrix Example 2

Decolonization	Africa	China
Violence	X	X
Poverty	X	X
Cultural identity	X	

Exhibit 4.2
Memorable Learning Experiences Activity
Start with the column on the left. List all memorable learning experiences you have had in the program. This is a brainstorm activity. Do not limit your responses! After completing the first column, answer the prompts in the subsequent columns.

PACE Learning Outcomes

1. Learner Understanding—Knowledge
2. Learner Facilitation—Application
3. Learning Environments—Knowledge
4. Learning Environments—Application
5. Professional Skills—Written and Oral Communication (what will be evaluated in your comps project), research/assessment techniques, use of technology

Memorable learning experience	What did you learn from this experience and why was it important?	Learning outcome category	Work sample/ artifact that would illustrate learning
Example: Learning styles inventory	I had never really thought that others might learn differently from myself. A real eye-opener.	Learner Understanding—knowledge (1) Learner Facilitation—application (2)	Learning style inventory results and reflection journal entry from ELP 568
Example: Prospectus for project	Writing has always been a weakness for me. Doing this assignment helped me improve my thinking and my writing.	Written communication (5) Research/ assessment skills (5)	Prospectus from ELP 520

in the program and then use the matrix to identify their learning and how it fits into the learning outcomes.

Activity suggestion: Mind maps. These are visual representations of connections that capture relationships between sometimes disparate chunks of information. They can be created on a computer using standard text software or specialized software. Or they can be created the old-fashioned way, with paper and colored pencils, markers, pens, and crayons. Whatever method students use, the idea is they can start with a concept in the middle and then radiate their ideas about the concept from the center of the map. For example, take World War II as the concept you want students to consider. Starting with World War II in the center, students might come up with background, people, politics, impact, and so on, and then add on more. Mind maps provide the opportunity to explore connections in a visual way versus textual, such as making an outline, and may actually help students make even more and deeper connections. In several of Candyce's classes, she tells students,

> A mind map is your individual account of something. . . . A mind map is structured; you are trying to let other people see a picture of what's going on in your head. Mind mapping (like other forms of writing and outlining) is a process: Working on the map may actually clarify, develop, or even change your ideas. A mind map is experimental. There is no single strand of perfection. Instead you are trying to open up ideas and find good working solutions to the problems or issues illustrated in the map.

Figures 4.1 and 4.2 illustrate what a mind map looks like and the ways it can be used.

Activity suggestion: Venn diagram. These diagrams show relationships between ideas. They were invented by John Venn in the 1800s and are used to indicate how things are related. We used two Venn diagrams previously in this book, Figures 3.1 and 3.2. Asking students to create Venn diagrams about related concepts is another form of reflection and helps students make connections. You can provide Venn

Figure 4.1
Mind Map Example 1

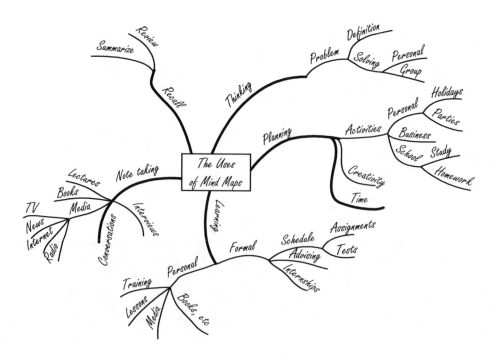

Figure 4.2
Mind Map Example 2

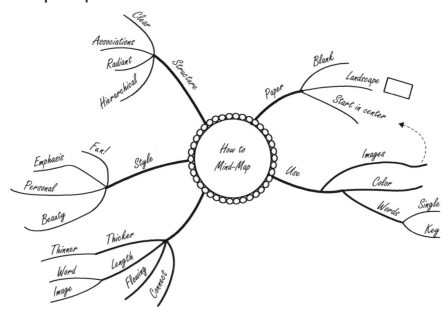

Figure 4.3
Venn Diagram Activity Example

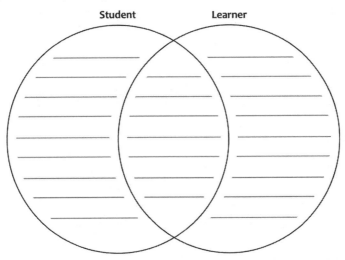

diagrams yourself and ask students to add the details. For example, give them the diagram in Figure 4.3 and ask them to list characteristics of a student, characteristics of a learner, and characteristics that overlap.

Activity suggestion: Consider alternative forms of written reflection. Reflection is usually written in the first person and from the perspective of one's own experience. In some instances, this might not be the most effective method for getting someone to reflect on an experience. Gillian Bolton (2010) argues that sometimes it is useful to take another's perspective. She has worked with people in helping professions (doctors, nurses, psychotherapists) to use reflective writing for improving practice. She conducts creative-writing workshops in which professionals write down an experience from a different perspective, such as that of a patient's family. The goal isn't to arrive at a true account of the experience but is instead an exploration of the experience, knowledge, and values of someone other than oneself. She also suggests writing poetry about an important event. This kind of creative writing can help one understand the perspective of others.

Make It More Complicated

Reflection is a skill, and as with all skills it takes time and practice to learn how to do something well. A way to help anyone learn new skills is to scaffold the learning of the skill. Scaffolding learning means that we provide a lot of support in the beginning of learning a task, and as students begin to master the task, we pull out the supports as they start to understand what they need to do and can meet (or begin to meet) the challenges we set out for them. Just as you would teach children in steps to learn to ride a bicycle, you can also do this in helping students learn to become reflective practitioners.

Activity suggestion: Start students out with simple and easy-to-answer reflection prompts as you begin this process. For example, you might begin a series of reflection assignments by asking students to describe what they know or have observed using who, what, and where questions. Subsequent prompts will become more complex and analytic once the students have mastered the ability to respond to this kind of descriptive prompt.

Learning Is Social: Make Reflection a Conversation

We often hear from faculty that they are excited initially about assigning reflective activities like a weekly journal but are ultimately disappointed by the results. They complain that the reflections are lackluster and without depth, and keeping a journal doesn't seem to be helping students perform better in class. On further exploration, we sometimes find that the faculty have not had any interaction with the students' journal throughout the term. Reflection is a communication process that requires an audience, and the audience for reflective writing is often oneself. Writing helps us get ideas, thoughts, and feelings out and provides us with an opportunity to clarify them. It would be great if all our students were self-directed learners who took full advantage of reflective activities, engaging fully and using what they discover in their learning. However, being our own audience may only go so far for many students. We all need to have an outside audience react to our communication to help keep the ideas flowing.

This is a reminder too that not all reflection is written. Reflection happens easily in class discussions, face-to-face, and online, especially if we provide discussion prompts that facilitate student reflection. It also helps to remind students that the discussion is actually a reflection activity. As part of the discussion process, take the time to let students think about what they have learned from the discussion.

Activity suggestion: Start a small-group discussion with a think, pair, share strategy. Ask students a question and let them think about it on their own and maybe jot down some notes. Then pair them with another student to discuss their observations and compare and contrast what they came up with. (Instead of a pair, it could be a small group.) Then ask them to summarize their findings and share them with the whole class. This provides students with the opportunity to reflect on their own but also benefit from other students' thinking.

Activity suggestion: Ask students to do a one-minute written reflection at the end of a class or small-group discussion that describes their thoughts before they entered the discussion, what they learned from others, and what they think now following the discussion.

For written reflections, make sure students receive feedback on most of the reflections they do in the course. It doesn't always have to be feedback only from you; it can be from friends, other students, or family.

Activity suggestion: Facilitate peer feedback. In asynchronous online discussions, it is common practice for students to share their thoughts, ideas, and feelings with a small discussion group and respond to at least two comments from peers. This can be done in a face-to-face class as well.

Of course, your feedback is important. Not only can you be the audience the students need to hear their thoughts, ideas, and feelings, but you also provide them with much needed guidance to help them think about and inform their ideas and help them focus their attention on areas they should explore further.

Because we value the reflective process, we often err by assigning a multitude of reflective assignments. However, if these reflections are not responded to in some way, they can lose their power. If you assign reflective activities, make sure to think about how to build in opportunities for a conversation about these reflections, either through your direct feedback, peer feedback, or discussion.

Activity suggestion: Use responsive reflection prompts. Vicki Reitenaur, an instructor in PSU's University Studies capstone program, uses responsive reflection prompts. She assigns a weekly or bimonthly reflection paper using a specific prompt. She responds minimally to the individual students' papers when she returns them; however, after reading all the papers for the assignment, she writes an open letter to the class outlining some of the themes that emerged from the students' papers. She speculates on what she has learned from reading these reflections and asks the students questions. These questions then provide the basis for her next reflection prompt. This strategy sets up a conversation about the ideas in the course and allows deeper reflection and understanding. Her responses are addressed in one document to the whole class, but she reads each paper and models the type of reflection she hopes her students will engage in.

Activity suggestion: Use generative knowledge interviewing. Melissa Peet (Peet et al., 2011) from the University of Michigan has developed a strategy she calls generative knowledge interviewing (GKI), which aims to help learners discover and express their tacit knowledge, and gives them a clearer and deeper understanding of their skills and abilities. Through this process, students can create a GKI ePortfolio. This story-telling process involves three learners. The first person tells three stories based on a theme, either broad or specific (e.g., three stories about learning or three stories about one's work as an engineer). The second person listens *generatively*, asking questions that elicit specifics about the storyteller's experiences, listening for themes that arise from the storytelling. The third person is an observer and note taker. Ultimately, the first person receives feedback from the listener and from the observer. To learn more about the process, go to https://sites.google.com/site/generativeknowledge/about-generative-knowledge-interviewing.

Activity suggestion: Facilitate peer review. The power of peer review should not be underestimated in facilitating reflection through feedback and conversation. Once students begin to create ePortfolios, peer review and peer showcases are especially effective. Students sharing with students not only allows them to give direct feedback, it also gives students an additional audience beyond the instructor (and often a more valued audience—their peers). While they might be willing to turn in a hastily written paper to the professor or show a lackadaisical ePortfolio when they submit it only to their teacher, students are often motivated to display their skills to their peers. And seeing other students' work, especially their working ePortfolios, gives students ideas about how they can improve their own. For example, one student may discuss a particularly significant class discussion that another student hadn't included in his or her ePortfolio; this could serve as a reminder that this discussion was also significant for the second student. Providing time for feedback and showcasing ePortfolios take advantage of the public nature of a digital medium.

CONCLUSION

Reflection is a complex process that educators have long recognized as an essential part of learning. While it is important to learning, it is also a difficult skill to teach and cultivate. This chapter provides definitions, suggests guiding principles for developing reflection activities in your class or program, and offers numerous ideas for activities to include or adapt in your courses.

CHAPTER 5

Making Connections or Integrating Knowledge

Judy's story: For the first few years I was in University Studies, I established and taught in our high school program, Senior Inquiry. In this program, we taught Freshman Inquiry to high school seniors in combined university–high school faculty teams. For one assignment, my teaching team chose three novels related to World War II. Since none of us had read one of the books, we asked a colleague at the high school, who had used that novel in another class, to lead the student group that chose that book. After one of their discussions, she asked the students why they liked the class so much. They told her they liked coming to class every day and dealing with different materials and loved making connections among the discussions and activities in the various fields. She said, "But you took American history and American literature as juniors last year. Didn't you make the connections then?" The students looked at her blankly and said no.

This story illustrates a common assumption educators have made for a long time that provides the basis for the distribution model of general education. The assumption is that if students take courses in the humanities, science, and social science, they will make the connections among the concepts and content they learn in those courses. However, although some students make the connections, most do not. In fact, when we brought faculty together to create the Freshman Inquiry teaching teams at Portland State University (PSU), we found that the faculty had not made the connections either and were surprised and delighted to discover them, just as the students were.

CONTEXT

When discussing ePortfolios and integrative learning, the term *making connections* will inevitably be part of the conversation. Connection is the nexus of the issue with integrative learning and with ePortfolios. As we discuss in Chapter 2, when we talk about making connections, we mean intentionally building relational links between prior understanding of material and the material that is currently being learned. Setting future goals and identifying needs to promote growth in understanding and use of material are part of making connections. The most straightforward way to achieve this linking is to create activities that ask students to find the relationship

- between assignments,
- between assignments and students' lived experiences,
- between courses in programs of study,
- among disciplines, and
- among assignments and experiences as they relate to the learning outcomes and goals for courses or programs.

The more students retrieve information from their memories and use it to make those connections, the deeper and longer lasting the learning will be (Halpern & Hakel, 2000). Also, as we discuss in Chapter 4, reflective practice is an important strategy to help students make those connections. We might even say that as learners, the way we connect learning and make it meaningful is through reflection. In this chapter, we provide examples of teaching methods and activities you can use as they are or as models for your own assignments and activities that ask students to create networks of their learning. We believe we need to design student experiences to make learning accessible and usable in their lives and careers and to help students develop those habits that will enable them to continue to pursue rich and lasting learning after graduation.

We first describe general classroom activities that allow students to do the mental work necessary to create an internalized understanding of what they have learned. This is followed by specific assignments and resources used at PSU that exemplify these general activities in practice.

Activity suggestion: Journals. Journals can take many forms. For example, in the sciences faculty use lab reports and include ending questions that connect experiments to class concepts and to scientific work in the world today. Humanities faculty use reflective journals as part of the ongoing structure of their classes. Weekly prompts ask students to think about what they have read and learned that week and to relate that learning in any number of ways to past understanding and to current events. It is important that the practice is regular and ongoing, and offers a structure that collects and demonstrates the students' growing understanding of the course material over time.

Activity suggestion: Reflection. In Chapter 4, we discuss reflective practice and offer ways of putting reflection into practice. Reflection can take several forms: verbal, written, or visual. In every form, it asks students to think about what they know and are now learning, and relate it to something to embed it into their ongoing and growing understanding of the material.

Activity suggestion: Mind maps. As we discuss in Chapter 4, mind maps are visual maps of assignments, ideas, concepts, and bits of knowledge that allow students to connect disparate activities and experiences to each other and to their past understanding. Mind maps are a graphical way to structure information, making the connections clear and helping students remember what they have done, capture their relationships, and generate new understanding and ideas. Mind mapping can be done individually or in groups, online using software, or on small pieces of notebook paper with pens and pencils or on large pieces of butcher paper with markers, colored sticky notes, crayons, and stickers. Students can bring laptops to class to create the mind maps in groups, or they can do it in a computer lab. Mind mapping is a critical thinking and reflective activity that is also an art activity. Maps can be simple or complex, rudimentary or very artistic.

Activity suggestion: Inventories of learning. Taking inventory is a list-making activity that provides an opportunity for students to catalog what they already know about a topic and determine what they need to know additionally. The list can include a self-assessment that allows students to formulate a plan for answering continuing questions, clarify areas of concern, and gain a more complete or accurate sense of certain material or course work. Students connect what they already know about a topic to what they are learning.

Activity suggestion: Scaffolding. As used in this book, scaffolding is designing a series of activities in a class so the students understand and learn to do a specific task. The scaffold is built using activities like immediate feedback, commenting, led discussions, and such. It is coaching students through the steps necessary to carry out a given task, such as research papers, and includes a series of activities to do the task well. These kinds of practices or supports for student learning are then removed as students learn what the expectations are for that activity or topic and can do them without support. Scaffolding can be ramped up to take on the next level of an endeavor until students achieve the level of understanding and capacity needed to direct and carry out their own activities, assignments, and goals. In other words, scaffolds are removed when the student understands what they were there to do.

As we discuss in Chapter 2 (see pp. 29–35), the Association of American Colleges and Universities (n.d.) initiated the VALUE project to define and create rubrics for what it considers the essential learning outcomes for college. The integrative learning rubric forms a guide that allows faculty to identify the kinds of connections they might look for and assign in their student work.

SPECIFIC ASSIGNMENTS AND RESOURCES

In the rest of the chapter, we provide examples of activities and resources to demonstrate how classroom practices can be used in different disciplines to give students experience in relating material and making their own meaning of it, in other words, an integrative learning experience. All work done in a class can be uploaded into an ePortfolio, then used to create a showcase ePortfolio to share with the class and family and for the program to use for program-level assessment.

Example 1

This example creates the opportunity for students to make the following connections: assignments to assignments, learning to personal life experience, assignments to program learning goals, and the summative or end assignment for the yearlong, three-course experience.

The portfolio assignment in Exhibit 5.1 is taken from the University Studies program at PSU. This assignment is the end-of-year version that all faculty use across the Freshman Inquiry level of the general education program. Faculty begin work on the portfolio during the first of three terms. Faculty can design how they introduce and build the portfolio experience that culminates in this project. Figures 1.1 and 1.2 are screenshot examples of the completed ePortfolio assignment.

Exhibit 5.1
Portland State University's Freshman Inquiry ePortfolio Assignment

INTRODUCTION

A portfolio is a compilation of your work that demonstrates skills, knowledge, and other qualities important to a particular field or course of study. To demonstrate your learning in Freshman Inquiry, you will create a portfolio to showcase and reflect on your achievements, your progress in the University Studies (UNST) goals, and how both of these connect to your larger educational goals and aspirations. Your portfolio should include a written reflection on each of the four UNST goals, at least ten different assignments completed during the entire year, and an essay discussing how you see your work in FRINQ connecting on your broader experience and aspirations in your major or career goals, as a member of your community (as you define it), as a citizen, or other important role.

PART 1: GOAL INTERPRETATION

For this section, write your interpretation and understanding of each of the four University goals and discuss how your work reflects progress in these goals:

- Communication
- Critical Thinking and Inquiry
- The Diversity of Human Experience
- Ethics and Social Responsibility

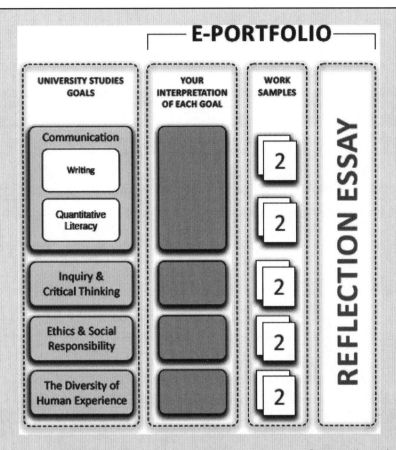

Below are several questions for you to consider in your reflection, but please do not simply list these questions and answer them. Include these answers in the natural flow of the overall commentary. See your instructor for details on length and format.

- In your own words, what does this goal mean? How does your interpretation differ from the UNST definition? [For a description of the UNST goals, go to www.pdx.edu/unst/university-studies-goals.] Have you changed or added to the UNST goal? If so, why?
- Are there concepts, ideas, and language that your FRINQ course used that you think fit this goal, but aren't reflected in the UNST definition? (In other words, if you were to write a definition of this goal for your class, what would it look like?)
- What role has this goal played in your learning this year?
- How is this goal relevant to your education in general? Have other classes and other experiences shaped your goal definition? How so?
- How is this goal relevant to life as a whole?

PART 2: EVIDENCE OF LEARNING AND GROWTH

For each goal, choose at least two of your own work samples from your FRINQ course that best demonstrate your progress. Include the original assignment sheet for each example, and discuss why you chose this work product to illustrate growth toward this particular goal:

- What specifically in the work product is the evidence? (Think in terms of passages, themes, insights, processes, experiences, etc.)
- What insights did you gain from doing this assignment? What part did you do particularly well/are most proud? Of which parts dissatisfied? If you were to do the assignment again, how would you do it differently?
- How might this assignment connect to other goals? Discuss how your this example of work could fit in other goals and why you ultimately chose to include it as evidence in this particular one.
- How does progress on this goal support your work in your major, your career aspirations, and your role as citizen in our society?

In addition to providing and commenting upon specific work samples, concern yourself with how you grew over the course of the term or year with respect to this goal. This can be done in a number of ways. For example, you might include multiple drafts of a single work (it would probably have to be a substantial one) and an accompanying discussion of insights that led to the revisions. Or, you could adduce multiple kinds of activities (assignments, in-class discussions, conversations with peers or the professor, mentor sessions) that all touch upon the same idea or theme and helped you develop ever greater appreciation for it.

PART 3: REFLECTION ON INQUIRY AND YOUR FUTURE

Write a two-page (750–1000 word) essay reflecting on your broader learning experience and goals. Questions to consider:

- What have been the most useful insights and highlights over the year in this class?
- What have you learned about your own academic goals and values over the year (in this and other classes)?
- As this class is titled Freshman Inquiry, how have you demonstrated inquiry in this class and in other learning contexts this year?
- What have you learned about your ability to contribute informed and original ideas into a professional/scholarly dialog/discourse/discussion?

- What decisions, resolutions, or next steps are you making in terms of your academic career here at the university?

As you write and shape your essay, think about how best to organize it. Does it make more sense to order the information chronologically? From most to least important point? From struggles to breakthroughs? In other words, your final essay shouldn't read like a free association. Revise and organize your essay into a logical order that best fits the points you are trying to make.

This reflection should be about what you learned, not about what you liked.

Note. From "2011–12 ePortfolio Assignment: Student Handout," by University Studies (n.d.), https://sites.google.com/a/pdx.edu/eportresources/frinq-eportfolio-assignment. Copyright 2014 by Portland State University, University Studies Program. Reprinted with permission.

Example 2

The faculty guide in Exhibit 5.2 assists connecting student work from inside and outside the classroom and among disciplines to program goals. This document helps faculty who teach Freshman Inquiry think about how to integrate the ePortfolio into their classroom. It is a guide to helping students make the connections among learning from their work in the course, the program goals, and their experiences outside the classroom.

Exhibit 5.2
Portland State University Freshman Inquiry Faculty ePortfolio Guide

IMPLEMENTATION TIPS & BEST PRACTICES

The following practices are not meant to be prescriptive. Indeed, this list will change as new ideas are practiced in the classroom and found effective.

SCAFFOLDING

- Include the UNST goals in your syllabus and discuss both the goal summaries and their rubrics sometime in the first few weeks of the course.

- Describe in class how you, the professor, see the first few class activities in relationship to the UNST goals. As time goes on, place increasing emphasis on how the students see this relationship.
- Consider adding small UNST goal-related, sub-assignments onto larger activities. For example, if you have assigned a response paper, ask the students to include at the end of the paper a single paragraph discussing such questions as:
  - Which of the UNST goals have you made most direct contact with in this assignment? How so?
  - Has your understanding of these goals changed in the course of this activity?
- Provide short real-world examples (news stories, videos) that illustrate successes or failures in the appreciation of the UNST goals.

USING MENTOR SESSIONS

- "Four hats" exercise: Divide students into four groups, one group per goal. Each group advocates for how their goal was central to a particular reading, assignment, or class activity. Create a panel of judges to award points based on the clarity and persuasiveness of advocacy.
- Ask individual students to give brief summaries of how their work addressed a goal.
- Peer review: Have students discuss how they see the work of their peers as illustrating progress toward a particular goal, or how a particular work product could do so more effectively.

PHASING

Fall term

- Create a website with a home page linking to four goal-specific subpages.
- Include an overall reflection or letter to the reader on the home page. This letter should address your thoughts on what you learned this term.
- Attach one assignment or work product to each goal.
- Write a one-paragraph (150–200 word) summary of what each goal means to you in the context of this class.

Winter term

- Organize the site to allow easy access to both Fall and Winter term work.

- Add to the diversity of work products used to illustrate progress toward each goal. (i.e. not just papers, but classroom and online discussions, group work, site visits, hands-on projects, etc.)
- Add discussions about why each piece is the best illustration of goal-related progress.
- Revise the overall reflection letter to the reader, guided by question prompts. (See student handout above for examples.)

Spring term

- Finalize the structure of the site to show how work has evolved throughout the year.
- Revise previous reflection essays into polished, coherent final versions. "Revision" here means much more than "edit"; it means "re-vision," to see anew what the form and substance of the document should be.

(Optional) Include links to or discussions of work from other courses.

Note. "FRINQ ePortfolio: Assignments and Resources: The Implementation Guide," by M. Flower, (n.d.), http://frinq-commons.michael-flower.com/commons/page2/portfolio.html. Copyright 2014 by M. Flower. Reprinted with permission.

Many faculty also ask students to design or choose images or icons to represent each goal. This part of the assignments gives students an experience in visual communication and the power of imagery. While Freshman Inquiry is a three-term course, the strategies for integrating learning can be replicated in single-term courses.

Example 3

This assignment connects assignment to assignment.
In a study of World War I in Senior Inquiry,

- we asked students to read poetry written in that time and about the experience of that war;
- we looked at early propaganda in film and print;
- we read novels written in the time about the war;
- we read historical accounts of key battles;
- we read political strategy and discovered why World War I was called the war to end all wars;

- we used several primary sources—diaries, letters, and newspaper articles;
- we looked at art of the time and had students create collages on specific themes and then had students present those to the class; and
- students had assignments required for each section of material. For example, they were asked to
  - summarize the article,
  - bring discussion questions to class meetings on the readings and films,
  - outline the history articles, and
  - write a research paper, the steps of which were assigned as part of the process of writing the paper.

The intent of all the assignments was to give students a view of the war that was more personal and included larger societal aspects. In most courses, students do a series of assignments and are expected to make the connections of ideas among the various readings and activities themselves, thereby integrating their learning into a cohesive system. Making a meaningful whole of disparate pieces of learning does not happen on its own. Students are leaving courses and programs without an overall understanding of the material and without making meaningful connections to ideas and understandings that are important to them as individuals. It is the "remember-the-material-for-the-test-only" syndrome.

If we want students to gain more comprehensive understanding and also to know and be able to replicate how they achieved that understanding in the future, we need to talk about relating material, model it, and assign activities that ask the student to do the mental work to make those connections.

To promote integrative learning, we include the following activities that ask students to do the mental work of making connections in the section on World War I:

1. Begin the section on World War I asking students to discuss what they already know about that time and about the war (inventory of learning).
2. Assign a journal entry or reflective prompt asking students to recall what they heard and remembered as a result of the previous discussion. The prompt is: "Summarize the discussion you had in class about WWI. Talk about what you brought to the discussion and any new information you gained participating in it. What questions remain that you want to investigate as part of our study of the war?" Collect the papers and save them until the end of the World War I study section.
3. At the end of the section of study, group students and ask them to create a mind map bringing together the various pieces they have studied. This process begins with students bringing all the work they have done in this section to class. Instructors hand out the student's first journal entry and ask students to reread the journal entry they wrote prior to the section on World War I.

Students then work together to create a mind map to detail what they now understand.

4. For the final piece, ask students to write a reflection on how their understanding of the war and its time has changed or has not, taking into account their mind map, their assignments, and their study of the war. Also, ask how their thinking about war in general might have changed. This ending assignment gives students time to step back and look at everything they have done on the subject and make the connections between what they knew or thought previously and relate the new information to it. This activity is essential in creating a more informed and lasting understanding of a topic.

All the work done can be uploaded into the ePortfolio available for later use in assessment, presentation, or transfer ePortfolios.

Example 4

In this assignment taken from business, students connect assignments to course goals and theory to practice in community-based learning. This example in Exhibit 5.3 was created by Jeanne Enders in the School of Business at PSU. It is from an organizational behavior course that is part of the business major. Enders teaches the course in an online format.

Exhibit 5.3
Organizational Behavior Course, Culminating Assignment

Course Outcomes—by the end of this course, you should be able to:

1. emulate some research skills used by organizational behavior (OB) researchers in the field
2. demonstrate recognition of the major OB issues and activities that organizations face
3. recognize a firm's OB practices/skills and the impact they have on organizational members
4. diagnose and solve some organizational behavior issues and problems regardless of functional specialty or industry
5. recognize your own OB practices/skills and the impact those skills have on others
6. demonstrate an ability to work interdependently and effectively in work groups and teams

The culminating project will address outcomes 1–4 in the following ways:

1. Students will locate two organizations, identify members of those organizations to approach to survey and will survey those organizational members on at least two occasions in order to learn about how OB principles work in those organizations.

2. Students will write up the results of their surveys in a way that others can understand and interpret what the student learned (report with reflection of learning).

3. The results will be matched with principles from the coursework (text, lecture, discussion, exercises) and potential effects of the practices in those organizations will be identified (mind map). Then, a paper will be written that uses the mind map to do a comparative analysis of two organizations along the dimensions of five self-selected dimensions of organizational behavior principles. These five principles will be determined after the student has interviewed members of the two organizations and has thereby identified the most relevant areas where comparisons and contrasts are the most significant for those organizations.

4. The student will develop a series of recommendations for the organizations and create an "executive summary" of the findings to share with the organizational members who participated in the study. Peer review feedback will be incorporated into this summary before releasing it to the survey participants (group reflection).

5. A culminating reflection will address outcomes 5–6 in the following ways:

   a. The student will evaluate team members on group work and provide constructive feedback to team members.

   b. The student will compose a reflection paper of approximately 3 pages in response to the feedback received from team members about their team performance.

   c. The student will compose a reflection paper of approximately 3 pages in response to assessments completed during the term about their own OB tendencies.

Example 5

The PSU social work program uses the following assignment:

- Midprogram assessment. Professionals from the community with faculty members assign case studies to predetermined groups of students. The students work to identify issues and create, as a group, a treatment plan to address those issues.

- Students present their findings and treatment plans to panels of community professionals and faculty members, who then evaluate the teams' presentations.

In this assignment, students apply understanding and knowledge from a series of courses and field experiences to an authentic case and work with professionals in the field to problem solve and evaluate their plans. This exercise introduces students, midway in their course of study, to working professionals and to how practice takes place in the field outside of academia. It allows students to begin forming networks for their future career goals.

Example 6

Science: connecting academic content to personal interests and life goals.

The example in Exhibit 5.4 is from Michael Flower's Science: Power-Knowledge class at PSU. He creates course websites that include links to various scientific controversies and student blogs. Flower asks students to research the controversies that interest them and capture their thinking as they develop through blogs and class discussions (see http://spk.michael-flower.com).

Exhibit 5.4
Science: Power-Knowledge Assignment Example

COURSE ASSIGNMENTS AND EXPECTATIONS

For many years now none of my courses have included exams—and this term will be no exception. Instead you will be asked to talk, write, talk and write some more; explore politicoscientific controversies; and generally contribute to our investigation of a number of lines of inquiry. That is, I am interested in seeing the ways you grapple with our readings and join in our discussions.

1. **Attendance (20%)**: It matters that you come to class. This is not a course for which you can "cram" at the last minute. As there are no exams, what would you be cramming for? Rather your work in the class must be ongoing. The course readings are challenging and require considerable discussion so as to establish how, in the aggregate, they support the lines of inquiry that are central to the course. The course assignments cannot be done well if you miss more than 2 or 3 class sessions; you will likely get lost in the underbrush of the arguments on the table.

2. **Critical reflections (20%)**: I am asking that you produce two reflections (due on January 29 and February 26), each of roughly 500 words. Reflections submitted late will be marked down so keep to the deadlines! As we read and discuss an increasing number of articles and book chapters, you will have the opportunity to interweave a growing array of intriguing and provocative ideas. The reflections are to be submitted as *either* Word documents *or* PDFs. I have set up a "delivery system" on the "Writing reflections" page of this site.

3. **Contributing to a quick class exploration of a controversy using Branch (10%)**: As an example of studying a controversy we will (as a class) look at a current debate about the significance of the Greenland ice sheet melt. You are asked to make a contribution to our understanding, prompted initially by a July 25, 2012 article in *The Washington Post*. Your postings should evidence the legwork you've done to advance our understanding of this controversy. This assignment will occupy a couple of weeks around the middle of the term and will involve the use of a new comment and discussion system called Branch. *You will need to have a Twitter account* to participate (Twitter is the mechanism used by Branch to connect participants to discussions). You might take a look at how Branch works before we begin using it. Your contribution(s) should be posted by Friday, February 15.

4. **Deploying and representing a politicoscientific controversy (50%)**: Having read and discussed a number of new ways to think about and characterize controversies, you are asked to tackle a controversy on your own (our approach being a version of what is done at a number of European universities, including Bruno Latour's institution in Paris, Sciences Po). You will submit two progress reports (due March 5, 5% and March 12, 10%) and the final submission of your project as either a website or a document using Word, Pages or other word processor capable of including photographs, tables and such (35%).

CONCLUSION

The examples in this chapter demonstrate practices that ask students to make intentional connections. The assignments are drawn from a variety of fields and courses and are meant to give you ideas for what you might do in your classes. Once you see what works for you and your students, you will be able to rethink your courses to include integrative learning and ePortfolios. These same kinds of practices can be used across courses to connect courses within a major as well as connect general education courses within the requirement and general education courses and goals to majors. It may be more important to help students transfer their learning from course to course than within a single course. As part of a larger assessment initiative, faculty in many departments have begun using curriculum maps to identify how their courses relate and teach the goals of the major. In these maps, the learning goals of the major are listed at the top of a table and the courses down the side. Each faculty member puts an X by each learning outcome for each course. This exercise is a wonderful way to begin talking about how the department wants to deliver its curriculum and where each outcome appears across the curriculum. Once program staff have completed the curriculum mapping process, departments can design an assessment plan for evaluating those goals (see Chapter 10).

CHAPTER 6

Making Connections for Lifelong Learning

As you are probably aware, integrative learning is very much tied up with the idea of lifelong learning. To be an integrative learner means that you are able *and* want to make connections over time and content areas. ePortfolio proponents (e.g., D. Cambridge, 2010) often talk about how ePortfolios can be used to promote lifelong learning, and, indeed, they allow students (and people in general) to be able to keep track of, assess, and consider their next steps in their learning journey. This chapter first focuses on three things to consider as you help students create an ePortfolio that promotes lifelong learning—engagement, metacognition, and taking risks—followed by suggestions for activities. While the first two chapters in Part Two focus on general classroom strategies to facilitate scaffolding, reflection, and making connections, this chapter and the next deal more with classroom strategies to help students create their ePortfolios.

ENGAGEMENT

It makes sense that engagement in a learning activity could lead to lifelong learning. If we are engaged, we are likely to become lifelong learners. And if we tend already to be lifelong learners, we will likely be engaged in what we are currently seeking to learn. However, as an instructor, you have the ability to have a direct impact on engagement. As much as we would like to wave a wand and make our students life-long learners, that will never happen. Thankfully, learning theory, particularly Ryan and Deci's (2000) self-determination theory, provides guidance for thinking about the process of engagement and how to facilitate it in our students.

The word *engagement* is thrown around a lot in higher education. A multitude of studies (e.g., Kuh, Kinzie, Schuh, & Whitt, 2010; Skipper & Argo, 2003) show that engagement is associated with many positive student outcomes, including retention, critical thinking skills, and self-directed learning, to name a few. Kuh (2009) defines *student engagement* as "the time and effort students devote to activities that are empirically linked to desired outcomes of college and what institutions do to induce students to participate in these activities" (p. 683). Chickering and Gamson (1987) offer seven principles for good practice in undergraduate education—student-faculty contact, active learning, prompt feedback, time on task, high expectations, respect for diverse learning styles, and cooperation among students—all of which align with engagement research. Kuh (2009) notes that "each of these represents a different dimension of engagement" (p. 684).

We use self-determination theory to frame our discussion of classroom practices for engaging your students in the process of making an ePortfolio. Reeve, Jang, Carrell, Jeon, and Barch (2004) define *engagement* as "the behavioral intensity, emotional quality, and personal investment of a student's active involvement during a learning activity" (p. 147). The following components characterize students who are engaged in their learning and in the development of their ePortfolios:

1. *Behavior:* Engaging in a learning activity requires attention, effort, and persistence. In a perfect world we would assign an activity such as creating an ePortfolio, and students would jump to attention, put forward their best effort, and resist the call of that volleyball game or worrying about their significant other and persist in finishing the assigned task. In an ideal world, an engaged student concentrates and stays on task (attention), invests his or her full self to the task (effort), and continues working on the task over time, even when facing difficulties (persistence).
2. *Emotion:* Students are much more likely to engage if they have an interest in an activity and enjoy the activity. In other words, they have to want to do the activity.
3. *Cognition:* Most activities involve more than just doing something. An engaged student is invested in completing the task and will think through what needs to be done, planning, implementing, and evaluating his or her progress.
4. *Voice:* Beyond just doing the activity, students who are engaged seek to influence the direction of the activity. This includes asking questions about the activity and expressing their preferences for completing the task.

These components seem rather obvious and seem to be all the things that happen in a student. While we don't have full control over student engagement, we do have control over how we structure our activities and how we motivate our students. To think about how to motivate and influence our student's engagement, we can learn from self-determination theory, which suggests that to influence student engagement, we need to provide a structure that helps students get started, keeps them going, and helps them finish up. In addition, we need to focus on tapping into what Reeve, Nix, and Hamm (2003) call one's *inner motivational resources*, or, more specifically, our students' interests, preferences, psychological needs, and internalized values. In other words, we need to support their autonomy in learning.

In this theory *autonomy* has a precise meaning and refers to "the inner endorsement of one's actions" (Reeve et al., 2003, p. 376). In order to fully engage students in their learning, self-determination theorists and researchers (e.g., Ryan & Deci, 2000) argue that we need to help students feel like they are choosing to engage.

Some or most of our classroom practices are focused on providing structure for our students; however, many of them are not centered on autonomy but are in fact focused on compliance. We assign a reading and give a quiz on the material to make sure they completed the assignment. We give grades on a paper based on a predetermined list of criteria. Our big-picture goal in the classroom may be to help students learn and develop a love of learning, but we often focus our energy on measuring what they have done and how they have complied. When so much of our energy (and theirs) is spent on compliance, it is no wonder our students' attention is focused on just making sure they do what we ask them to do. Assignments and grading certainly provide structure, but without a shared focus on supporting autonomy in learning, we may not get to our ultimate goal of promoting lifelong learning. While the assignment of an ePortfolio has great potential in promoting autonomy in one's learning, it can be just another assignment if we aren't conscious about the activities we ask students to participate in.

Self-determination theory provides some suggestions for providing an appropriate structure and for supporting autonomous learning. We discuss the structures that support autonomy and learning here as well as provide some specific activities.

STRUCTURE

To think about using structure in the same breath as talking about supporting autonomy may seem like a contradiction. However, the structure we are talking about is the foundation one needs to be able to act autonomously, and it also helps set students up for the next factor supporting the development of lifelong learning, metacognition. Our recommendation is that you think about providing specific kinds of structure at three points in the student's development of the ePortfolio. First, provide students with guidance in getting started. Second, provide structure to motivate and help them to keep going. Third, provide structure toward the end to help them complete the project. Each of these points in time demands a different kind of structure.

Activity suggestion: At the beginning students need a lot of structure. They need clear directions as well as a sense of how much time it will take to complete the project. This is especially true for a multilayered, complex project such as an ePortfolio. What are the steps students should take? What is your suggestion about where they should start? What are the challenges they might face in building their ePortfolio? What have the students experienced? Distributing a handout of frequently asked questions when you assign the ePortfolio can help students anticipate problems they might not have thought about at the beginning and give them the tools to confront any difficulties. These tools can help our students be autonomous learners.

It is also helpful to provide students with a timeline and checkpoints to keep them on target. This can be associated with assessing their work periodically or asking them to assess their own or each other's work. Speaking of assessment, it is also good to tell your students what your expectations are in evaluating their work. How many points is the ePortfolio worth? What are the standards to measure their success? Give them a rubric that shows how you will evaluate the ePortfolio (see Chapter 10 for more on rubrics). Some incentive to complete the work is needed, especially in the beginning, when they may not see how rewarding creating an ePortfolio might be. An external reward, such as a grade, can be a start in helping students get to the point of feeling like they are choosing to engage in the project versus just doing the project because they have to.

If all this sounds like what you would do when you assign any project, you are right. However, you can do some things in the beginning to tap into a student's autonomy. One is to make a connection between the project of the ePortfolio and students' own personal goals and aspirations. Providing examples of ePortfolios and telling the creator's story or inviting a former student to describe the process of creating the ePortfolio can be inspiring and help students make connections to their own experience. Being explicit about the learning goals you hope your students will be able to work on is helpful. Stating these goals on your learning objectives in the syllabus or on the written assignment might seem like enough. But the important ones need to be highlighted and discussed.

Last, inviting students to make connections between their own personal goals and the goals of the ePortfolio assignment is motivating. You can use the opening letter assignment described on pp. 62–64 in Chapter 4 and ask students to go back to their letters and compare their goals with the goals of the ePortfolio. Review these letters yourself, and as you introduce the ePortfolio assignment, remind students that many of their personal goals are similar to the goals of the ePortfolio assignment. You might even be surprised how similar students' individual goals are to the ePortfolio assignment.

It is easy to assume that once students are given clear instructions and appropriate guidance they will then be successful in completing the project. And since we are talking about autonomy, we should just leave them alone, right? According to Reeve et al. (2003), particular kinds of support are needed in the middle of a project to help students remain engaged and move forward. They suggest that reminders, encouragement, and feedback are useful strategies at this point. We have found peer review, which provides all these supports, especially useful.

Activity suggestion: Peer review of ePortfolios. Peer review serves several purposes: It helps students stick to a timeline, as certain parts of the ePortfolio are due at a certain time; it conveys the message that the ePortfolio is important enough to use classroom time; it provides an opportunity to get feedback from peers; and it provides students with an opportunity to see their peers work and to learn from them.

This last point is especially important, and our experience is that it contributes a great deal to students' continued engagement. Seeing their peers' ePortfolios exposes them to multiple representations of what works and what doesn't in an ePortfolio (e.g., an animated dancing elf probably isn't appropriate in a professional ePortfolio). It also helps them think about and reconsider what they have included in their ePortfolio. They may have forgotten about one of the class's written assignments that would be a great artifact for a particular learning outcome demonstration, they may make a connection between how pictures and text can be used well with each other, or they may learn a technology trick they didn't know before.

In our experience of doing peer reviews of ePortfolios, our biggest surprise is how engaged students become during this process, which is one of the rare times in the academy when students get to interact with their colleagues in a formal academic setting. They are sharing an academic product, much like doing a presentation on an idea, but it is about them, so they are concerned about how they appear to others. An ePortfolio, while intrinsically personal, is also public. Sharing ePortfolios uses the public nature of the ePortfolio, which aids in their engagement and learning. This is when we hear students assessing their own work honestly and openly. Students are in the feedback role, critically analyzing their peers' work. And they get incredibly excited in discussing each other's portfolios, with comments such as, "Look at what I did here"; "This connection is really cool"; "Is it okay to use this picture here?"; "How did you do that?"; "That looks really great"; and "How did you think of that?" The following are some guidelines for this activity:

1. Do a peer review midway through the project. A significant amount of work should be assigned prior to the review so that students have something substantial to share.
2. Make an event of it. Have a potluck or bring snacks for the class. It is special to share students' work and acknowledge their accomplishments.
3. Make sure you leave enough time for the event. While it might initially feel like you might be taking away time from the content of the course, the benefits of doing this will outweigh any concern.
4. Provide a structure of sharing and commenting, for example:
   a. Give each student a length of time to present. Students should display each web page and highlight items on the page.
   b. Ask students who are presenting to indicate what parts of the ePortfolio they are proud of, what they like or what works for them. This is an opportunity to engage in self-assessment.
   c. Instruct students to ask for specific feedback, again taking advantage of engaging in self-assessment. For example, one might say, "I didn't have enough time to figure out what picture I wanted to represent this page. Any ideas?" Or another might ask a more technical question: "How do you change the background cover on this page?" Asking students to do this

helps them think critically about their work before they present it (and get the feedback they need).

   d. In giving feedback, students should practice providing respectful critiques. We have found it useful to have students respond to the questions the presenting student has asked and then

     i. tell the student what they liked,

     ii. offer ideas for improving the ePortfolio, and

     iii. ask if they can take an idea and use it in their own ePortfolio.

   e. Finally, the critique of an ePortfolio should end with one more reflection from the presenter: What will the presenter take from the critique? What has he or she learned?

5. Provide feedback to students yourself. Don't lock yourself out of the process, but wait until the students have given their feedback to their peers.

Endings are hard, and we don't always take the time to properly end a learning activity. In passing over or rushing through the ending of an assignment, we miss the opportunity to reflect on what was learned and what can be carried forward in our next endeavors (relationships, future courses, assignments).

So again we talk about reflection, which is important for any ending, although it may be one of the last things we want to do. In the end, we are usually ready to move on, and this is why it is important to structure reflection, which can be structured in many ways for an ePortfolio, into our assignments.

Activity suggestion: Conduct an ePortfolio showcase. An ePortfolio showcase at the end of the course asks students to present their assessment of their work as well as what they learned from doing the activity. A short reflective essay may be assigned in conjunction with the ePortfolio assignment in which students comment on what they learned and say how they might continue to use the ePortfolio. The particular structure is not as important as making sure you do something that encourages students to engage in the process of creating, managing, and concluding a project with reflection. Having opportunities to participate in this process (preferably more than once in their academic career) gives them practice in being autonomous learners. They can use the skills of creating, managing, and ending with reflection in all their life's work.

Rewards such as grades and feedback are important structures to provide students at the end of a project like an ePortfolio. Of course, we do these things already. Courses and assignments almost always end with a grade and some feedback, but we want to remind you that these structures matter. To help students become autonomous learners, they need to be rewarded for their efforts and be given feedback about what they have done well and how they could improve. Table 6.1 shows the kinds of structure we might provide in each phase of a project such as an ePortfolio.

Table 6.1
Types of Structure

At the Beginning	In the Middle	At the End

Goals
Directions
Expected challenges
Incentives
Timelines
	Reminders
	Encouragement
	Peer review (modeling,
	  feedback, and praise)
		Opportunities for
		  reflection
		Rewards
		Feedback

METACOGNITION

Another factor involved in promoting lifelong learning is the development of meta-cognitive skills. Metacognition described simply is our ability to think about think-ing. Specifically, it is understanding what we know, what we don't know, how we learn, and how we manage ourselves. We explain this in more detail in the next paragraph, but understanding our learning process will help us engage in lifelong learning, motivating and guiding us as we develop and grow. This section provides some ideas on metacognition, the role of the ePortfolio in developing skills, and ideas for assignments geared toward promoting metacognition.

Metacognition is defined by Flavell (1979) as "cognition about cognitive phe-nomena" (p. 906) or more simply as thinking about thinking. Flavell and others (e.g., Scheid, 1993; Sternberg, 1986) have researched and written about this overarching concept and identified two basic parts of metacognition: knowledge about our think-ing (or what Flavell and others call *cognitive knowledge*) and regulation or control of our thinking.

Cognitive knowledge has to do with knowing oneself as a learner and under-standing the factors that affect one's thinking. For example, when I approach study-ing for a test in a course, I am able to think about what I need to study and how I should approach my studying, select a strategy I think might work, and as I'm study-ing consider if I understand what I'm studying and if I am ready to move on to the next task. Because I believe that if I study long and hard enough I will understand the concept, I keep studying even when I'm tired. My roommate, however, thinks it is all about being born smart, so he stops studying when he gets distracted.

Regulation or control of our thinking involves the ability to set goals, using knowledge and skills one already possesses, and budgeting one's time. So in my study example, I have a goal of getting at least a B on a test. I set aside a little bit of time each day to study for this test, and as I study I realize that what I learned in a course last term is relevant to what I am studying now, so I look at my test from that course to help me study for this course. I have identified, selected, and used the strategies and resources I need to be successful.

Obviously, not all students have such metacognitive skills. In fact, many of our students do very little thinking about their own thinking. And while we all agree that employing metacognitive skills is important for helping us learn and be successful, very likely we spend little time directly addressing it with our students. In essence, metacognition is a part of integrative learning—incorporating one's understanding of one's learning into a task. As with integrative learning, we often expect students to know how to do this, but they need experience in developing metacognitive skills.

ePortfolios can be a rich tool for aiding students in the development of metacognitive skills. In fact, the process of creating an ePortfolio is indeed a metaphor for metacognition. Making an ePortfolio requires students to think about their thinking. While creating an ePortfolio parallels what is required for metacognition, we can more directly encourage this through activities and assignments in the classroom and in students' reflections in their ePortfolios.

PROMOTING COGNITIVE KNOWLEDGE

We encourage you to have your students consider two parts of cognitive knowledge: their general knowledge and beliefs about thinking and learning, and understanding their own learning.

Our beliefs about learning and how to think drive how we operate in the world. If we believe that our success is determined primarily because of our raw intelligence, we will put little effort into learning something because doing so really won't make a difference. However, if we believe that almost anything is possible to learn with effort and in time, we are more motivated to continue to work at learning before or if it becomes challenging. This belief in incremental learning allows students to continue even when they are discouraged, and research has shown that these students are ultimately more successful in grades and persistence in higher education and also in the real world of work (e.g., Bransford, Brown, & Cocking, 1999; Dweck, 1999). While we can acknowledge innate skills and abilities, we know from decades of cognitive research that those who put in the effort ultimately can learn. However, many of our students are entity learners, believing that they are good in math but bad at writing. While they may be assessing themselves accurately in the moment, this assessment doesn't motivate them to put an effort into learning how to do something better because they believe it won't ultimately make a difference.

Activity suggestion: Read about learning. We have found it helpful to ask our students to read summaries of the research that shows that learning is actually incremental and based on innate talent. We have found Tagg (2000, 2004) and Leamnson (2002) to be particularly useful.

Activity suggestion: Ask students to complete a learning autobiography. The following assignment can be adapted to meet the needs of your class.

Think about a time that you learned something new and became, if not proficient, at least pretty good at it. Write about how you learned this new activity or idea in a three- to five-page paper. What did you need to do to learn this? What steps did you take? Did the activity or idea seem to come naturally and require little effort? If so, why do you think it came easy? Or did it take great effort to learn? If so, describe how you motivated yourself to continue. Think about your experience in the context of one of these articles: Tagg (2000, 2004) or Leamnson (2002). Does your experience support or negate the ideas in the article? Why? Students typically learn a great deal from this exercise whether it results from an in-class discussion or a paper. Even those who argue that their innate abilities accounted for their ability to master something new, they acknowledge that effort played some role in learning and mastering it. Students always bring up that persistence in learning is accompanied by some kind of motivation to learn—typically a passion (e.g., skateboarding) or doing something that had meaning or consequence (e.g., learning precalculus to pass the advanced placement test to get into the college of their choice).

Activity suggestion: Remind students of their discoveries from these assignments throughout the course. Do they get stuck writing a paper required for the course? Remind them to think about what they learned from this assignment that will help them move forward. Are they wondering about the relevance of a particular assignment (maybe even the ePortfolio)? Remind them of the purpose and meaning of the assignment and ask them to connect that to their ultimate goal in taking the course. Invariably, students list this assignment in their reflections in their ePortfolios as one of the key learning activities of the course.

PROMOTING SELF-KNOWLEDGE

Another kind of metacognition we can promote is thinking about one's thinking.
Activity suggestion: Use these prompts for written reflection or in-class discussion:

- What do students know about a topic/idea/activity, and what do they need to know to continue?
- What steps do they need to take to be able to complete this assignment?
- How do they achieve a goal (e.g., decreasing the number of comma splices in a paper)?
- What did they learn from this assignment that will take them forward to the next assignment or course (e.g., ask them to write in one paragraph at the end of the paper they turn in, what they learned about their writing process that they want to remember when writing the next paper)?

As you can see, the potential prompts are endless. We should do anything we can to help students think about their thinking. Engaging in this kind of reflection early and often also helps students learn to ask themselves these kinds of questions as a habit, thus leading to habits for lifelong learning. An ePortfolio assignment promotes this kind of self-knowledge by asking students to reflect on what they have learned. Providing the space for students to take time to think about how and what they have learned creates a space for metacognition.

MAKING RISK OKAY

To promote lifelong learning, we need to help students understand and experience risk. We cannot take on new adventures in business, relationships, or civic interactions without inviting at least a minimal amount of risk. Opening ourselves up to new experiences and thus new learning entails risk, either by making mistakes or by provoking disagreement.

Any new endeavor involves risk, even if a minor one. I buy expensive yarn and start knitting a new scarf, but I might not finish it or I do a lousy job and never wear it, making the purchase a waste. Or I call the person I met on the bus who gave me his card and ask to meet for an interview about what I think might be my dream job, and he might forget who I am and hang up the phone. To make something happen, to learn, we must take a risk.

In the classroom this means we need to create an environment that not only encourages risk taking in learning but also values it. We can do this in several ways, one of which is creating a space where one can take risks safely without fear that things will go utterly crazy and that no learning will happen. Students need to know that you, the instructor, know about the subject you are working on together, and while you will be allowing students to explore a topic and make mistakes in learning, you have enough knowledge and organizational skills and planning to bring them back to what is ultimately important. They need to understand that you can manage *planned* chaos.

Activity suggestion: Provide the structure for the ePortfolio assignment and be clear about what is expected. However, the design, what they choose to upload as evidence for your learning outcomes, and the illustrations they use should be up to them. Believe us, they will make mistakes, but the great thing about ePortfolios is they are not static. Mistakes can be fixed relatively easily because of the digital medium. When one gets to experiment, however, and learn what works and what doesn't work by doing it versus being told how to do it, the learning is much deeper. Also, the student then has the experience of trying something, seeing it go wrong, and being able to correct it. Sometimes, today's mistakes are tomorrow's gems.

In creating an ePortfolio, students can also develop new ideas and thoughts about themselves. They can take a risk to present themselves in different ways as they consider the audience for the ePortfolio. In creating ePortfolios, students often describe seeing themselves in a new light, sometimes marveling in seeing what they know and understand when they look at their own ePortfolio as an observer. When we take risks, we can sometimes learn new things about ourselves that we can carry forward into the future.

Activity suggestion: Model vulnerability. Perhaps ironically, it is also important to show your own vulnerability and not be afraid to make mistakes and model how to manage those mistakes. Being transparent about making mistakes or not knowing something students ask you shows students that you too are engaged in the process of learning. We often end up not being able to answer students' technology questions about their ePortfolios. This is a time to model resourcefulness and willingness to ask for help. Sure, it is a little embarrassing to be unable to answer a student's question right away, but managing our lack of knowledge teaches the student an important lesson about being willing to take a risk.

Most important, we need to provide students with the opportunity to take risks and not fear harsh evaluation. The scaffolding activities we've talked about throughout the book so far are extremely important. In-class activities that help students practice or play with ideas we want to see demonstrated in the ePortfolio provide students with the opportunity to experiment before the final product is due.

CONCLUSION

In closing, ePortfolios are a great tool to promote lifelong learning. They provide opportunities for students to engage more directly with their learning. Building an ePortfolio in the context of a class or program also models the process we use in taking on and managing new and complex tasks, and it provides opportunities for students to try new ideas.

Chapter 7

Communicating Effectively in ePortfolios

A Picture Is Worth a Thousand Words

The convergence of media and technology in a global culture is changing the way we learn about the world and challenging the very foundations of education. No longer is it enough to be able to read the printed word; children, youth, and adults, too, need the ability to both critically interpret the powerful images of a multimedia culture and express themselves in multiple media forms. (Thoman & Jolls, 2004)

Candyce's story: In summer 1997, while reviewing ePortfolios for program assessment for University Studies, I found myself getting increasingly annoyed. I was looking at the clock repeatedly, wondering when I could get out of the room. My eyes were starting to go out of focus and they were beginning to burn. While I had looked forward to participating (and not just for the free lunch and minimal stipend) in our assessment review as it was the first year that we were going to see student ePortfolios, I now realized that we had a long way to go as a program in implementing ePortfolios in our Freshman Inquiry program. Students were clearly excited by using the web to represent their work. Unlike the paper portfolios we were used to reviewing, which were organized quite similarly—having tabs to separate topics, beginning with an introductory essay, and including artifacts after the essay—the ePortfolios were all really different. Students seemed to like using the visual medium in their ePortfolios. Unfortunately, they needed to learn how to use the visual aspects appropriately. Animated cartoon characters moving across the top of the web page, yellow text on a black background, spinning letters spelling out the student's name were not the things we were hoping to see. Who do they think is looking at and evaluating their work?

As we often hear, the medium is the message (McLuhan, 1964), and this is especially true in an ePortfolio as well as in other kinds of student work. If a student turns in a handwritten, wrinkled, unbound 10-page essay, we undoubtedly make a judgment about the student's seriousness and skill. While it is not enough to turn in a well-polished, edited, appropriately bound and labeled paper, doing so provides a frame for how an instructor approaches and thinks about the student's work. As an ePortfolio encompasses visual and text-based messaging, the possibilities of making a mistake in communicating what one has learned increases exponentially. In light of this reality, this chapter discusses the concept of digital presence and digital identity, its importance, and the role of the ePortfolio in establishing one's digital identity. We also discuss how to approach teaching students about creating their ePortfolios, keeping visual and textual considerations in mind, as well as how to integrate these mediums in the ePortfolio. Last, we provide some activities to help you implement these ideas in your classroom.

DIGITAL PRESENCE

In today's web-dominated culture it is virtually impossible not to have some kind of web presence. This is true not only for our younger, more tech-savvy (or as least social-media-savvy) students but also our older returning students. Websites such as Facebook and LinkedIn, and blogging sites (Blogger, Wordpress, Tumblr) are widely used. Our names and sometimes photos are easily searchable with Google or other search engines. Whether we like it or not, this digital content is often part of the first impression we make on our current and future friends, colleagues, and employers. In fact, our digital presence can either facilitate or doom our job searches and maybe even potential romantic interests. As students move from collegiate into more professional spheres, their online presence and digital identity become even more important.

Students need to learn to manage their presence on the Internet and make sure it matches who they are and what they hope to portray. ePortfolios help students manage their digital presence by creating a digital identity that reflects their values, skills, and accomplishments. Because of the versatility of the ePortfolio, students can create one or more ePortfolios that can be used for a variety of purposes and appeal to a wide variety of audiences.

ePortfolios by definition provide a space to display a student's experiences, accomplishments, and reflections. Figure 7.1 illustrates how a digital presence can be viewed.

The center of the Venn diagram represents the ePortfolio, the intersection of evidence of experiences and accomplishments and reflection in a digital medium. In creating an ePortfolio, students have the ability to master all three of these areas. Other forms of a web presence offer a more limited view of an individual; for example, Facebook is only a digital presence, a blog is digital and contains reflection, and a LinkedIn profile combines digital evidence of experiences and accomplishments. Finally, without the digital component, a paper portfolio can be a combination of reflection and evidence of experiences and accomplishments.

An ePortfolio provides a deep and rich way of demonstrating one's identity in a digital format and can also help in the development of one's identity in general. Being asked to present ourselves digitally allows us to consciously think about who we are, what we value, how we demonstrate what we know, and what makes us unique. The

Figure 7.1
Digital Presence

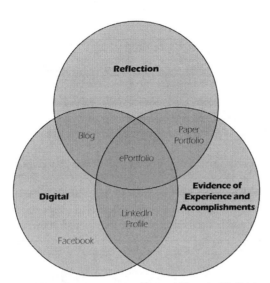

Note. From *Walking the ePortfolio Talk: Begin Your Portfolio in 4 Hours,* by W. Garrison, July 2013, workshop presented at the meeting of the Association for Authentic, Experiential and Evidence-Based Learning, Boston, MA. Copyright 2013 by Wende Garrison. Adapted with permission.

ePortfolio provides the opportunity for students to control their digital identity by building and managing what others see on the Internet. Later in this chapter, we provide an example of a digital presence and identity activity.

Part of the educational benefit of an ePortfolio is that it provides an opportunity for students to think about communicating information for specific purposes and to specific audiences. Being able to do this is integrative learning—making a connection between what we know and how to effectively communicate. Learning how the delivery of information affects our audience's ability to engage with the material and understand information is a lifelong tool.

WHAT IS THE PURPOSE? WHO IS MY AUDIENCE?

As with any form of communication—a paper for an English class, an Instagram photo, a thank-you card to your grandmother, a status update on Facebook—an ePortfolio has a purpose and an audience. We need to tailor the delivery of our communication based on the purpose and audience of our ePortfolios. Identifying the purpose and audience of the ePortfolio is one of the first steps your students should take as they begin to work on the design of their ePortfolios. They may have some ideas about what they want to upload (including required assignments), but thinking about how they want to present themselves may not be as obvious.

If you have assigned creating an ePortfolio in your class, you may think that the purpose is obvious: Students need to do it to get a grade. However, we know that you have assigned it for a purpose beyond that and have likely explained what the purpose is in your syllabus and in class presentations. As we discuss in Chapter 6, the more students are able to engage with the material, the better they integrate what they are learning. Ask students to think about the purpose of the ePortfolio assignment beyond just doing it for a grade.

While the primary audience is the faculty member who assigned the ePortfolios, the audience is much broader: fellow students, perhaps an academic adviser, and possibly future instructors. Even if students do not show their ePortfolios to people other than the instructor, having students think about that audience of one can be instructive and help them develop integrative learning skills. Later we provide a few classroom exercises that help students begin to explore the question of purpose and audience.

COMMUNICATION STRATEGIES IN THE EPORTFOLIO

Two of the primary differences between hard-copy and electronic portfolios are visual expectation and effect. Hard-copy portfolios tend to contain only written text, and art portfolios tend toward the visual, with little or no text. ePortfolios fall in the middle with a combination of the visual and textual, offering students the opportunity to understand and practice multimedia communication.

As your students begin to develop their ePortfolios, it is important to help them recognize that they are employing multiple communication strategies beyond text and visuals. They are writing text, they are using visual communication through the design of the ePortfolio and through images they include, and they may even be using audio or video files. It is not enough to just upload those A-plus papers. Good communication using these techniques in their ePortfolios means that students need to consider what they include, how they include these elements, and the impact they have on their audience. Thinking about design issues and what these decisions communicate is an important step.

CONSIDERING DESIGN ISSUES IN CREATING THE EPORTFOLIO

Every ePortfolio has a web architecture that allows the reader to navigate through the ePortfolio, just as you do with any website. You may provide students with a template, but even with a template students have many decisions to make in how they present information in their ePortfolio. (We discuss templates later in this chapter.)

Students should consider the following regarding the design of their ePortfolio (with or without a template). You could use this as a handout for students or when you give students feedback about their ePortfolios. These suggestions are adapted from Portfolio to Professoriate (n.d.):

ePortfolio Design Hints

- Think about what you put in the URL: For a student learning ePortfolios, it is probably best to use his or her name. MyPortfolio, MyFirstYear, FinalPort does not provide specific information. Titles such as ryansportfolio are also not as professional or clear as simply using ryanjones. If the name is taken, add a middle initial or pick a shorter variation, and avoid hyphens or numbers.
- Think about what each page on the ePortfolio looks like:
  - Include white space. Reading online is difficult if web pages are just a long series of text. It is helpful to have white space between paragraphs and text and illustrations to break up text. Boag (2011) said research shows there are several advantages to adding white space in web pages:
    - makes reading more legible
    - increases comprehension of what one is reading
    - increases attention to the most important elements on the page
    - communicates elegance, openness, and freshness
  - Include a relevant illustration or two on each page; text only is not very welcoming or compelling. Adding an illustration breaks up the text and gives the viewer a better idea of what the page is about.
  - Use your own photos wherever possible. Not only does this personalize the page, you will avoid mistakes in attribution. If you use illustrations that you have taken from the Internet, make sure you cite them appropriately and include the URL.
  - Think about your writing. Use short sentences and short paragraphs. Consider using bulleted lists when appropriate on your pages. The links you create can lead to conventional academic documents, but your ePortfolio pages should be an introduction to these documents and be inviting enough to make your readers want to click on that link.
  - Make sure your welcome statement is clear. Let your reader know what your ePortfolio is about. Remember, use white space, illustrations, and short sentences and paragraphs.

USING EPORTFOLIO TEMPLATES

Faculty and program administrators often create templates for their students to use in building an ePortfolio. We talk more about the structure and creating ePortfolio templates in Chapters 8 and 9. Templates can provide the basic architecture for students' ePortfolios, helping them organize their work and present it in a way that viewers know where to find what they are looking for. When ePortfolios are going to be used for program or institutional assessment, a common template for students can be helpful. Without a template, it could be difficult for an assessor to find what he or she needs to assess.

However, there is a danger in overdoing an ePortfolio template for students. If the ePortfolio template is merely a fill-in-the-blank form, students may have little ability to make it their own. They may find it hard to integrate the content of their ePortfolio with how they choose to communicate it, and if the format of the ePortfolio is already laid out for them, they don't get the experience of determining how to shape and present their digital identity.

As we discuss in Chapter 8, some platforms designed primarily for assessment leave little leeway for students to do much more than fill in reflection prompts and upload documents. Again, using this highly precise format doesn't allow students to struggle and learn from thinking about how their communication strategies affect their audiences.

ACTIVITIES TO FACILITATE COMMUNICATION IN EPORTFOLIOS

The following activities can help students learn about their digital presence and identity, think about the purpose and audience for their ePortfolios, and help them apply good design principles.

Activity suggestion: Digital Presence and Identity Activity. The activity in Exhibit 7.1 can be a homework assignment or used in a class setting and discussed as a group, or both. The purpose is to raise awareness of one's digital identity and the message it gives to the audience.

Activity suggestion: ePortfolio Purpose and Audience Analysis Assignment. The activity in Exhibit 7.2 could be a class discussion or a homework assignment.

Activity suggestion: Critical Analysis. Having students look at a variety of websites with a critical eye can be very helpful. This can be either a homework assignment or an in-class lab activity. We have found this to be most effective when done in a lab. Students can share their results and learn from each other. Have your students look at three to five websites of their choice. They can be ePortfolios you have shown students, but we like at least one of the sites they review to be one they visit at least weekly.

Have them analyze the site using the ePortfolio design hints on p. 105. What guidelines have been followed? What guidelines have been ignored? How does this work for the overall effectiveness of the site? What message does the design of the site give the reader?

Have them think about who they think the primary audience is for the site. Why did the site designers make the choices they made given the presumed audience?

Have your students end with a conversation about what they want to take away from this experience and use in their own ePortfolios.

Exhibit 7.1
Digital Presence and Identity Activity

Introduction: This activity will help you learn about your online presence and help you begin to think about building your own digital identity with your ePortfolio.

Instructions:

1. Google yourself. In addition, use another search engine like Yahoo or Bing to note any differences. List the top 5 websites that are identified below and identify what kind of site is each one is:*

Website	Type of Site

Here is an example search result:

Website	Type of Site
Portland State University	Education/place of employment
LinkedIn	Professional/social media
Google Images	Pictures
Facebook	Social media
Out of Practice	Professional association

2. Given the search results, without looking at the content of the sites, what do you think someone who did not know you would say about you as a person?
3. Looking at the content of the sites, what do you think someone who did not know you would say about you as a person?
4. If you were to Google yourself in 5 years, what sites would you hope to find? What would the content in these sites say about you?
5. Bonus question: Do a Google search on an individual you admire and complete questions 1–3 with your results.

*If you do not have five search results, it means you don't have much of an online presence yet. If that is the case, skip ahead to question #4 and answer it.

Exhibit 7.2
ePortfolio Purpose and Audience Analysis Assignment

Introduction: It may seem obvious what the purpose of your ePortfolio is and who the audience is. You will be getting a grade for your ePortfolio! And, the audience is your professor. However, the potential for your ePortfolio is immense if you can imagine it. This exercise will help you examine the use of your ePortfolio and analyze the audience for your ePortfolio.

Purpose of your ePortfolio:
Brainstorm what this or an ePortfolio derived from the one used in this course could be used for (with some ideas to start you out):

    To get a good grade in this class
    To serve as a basis for an online resume
    To document my learning through college
    To let people back home know what I'm doing in college

Audience for your ePortfolio:
Choose at least 3 purposes you brainstormed above and put them in the first column. Then brainstorm who might be the audience for the purpose you identified.

Purpose	Potential Audience
Example: good grade in class	*Professor X*

Now for each audience you have identified, use the following to analyze your audience:

A: Analysis: Who is the audience? (You've done this one already.)
U: Understanding: What does the audience know about the subject of this ePortfolio?
D: Demographics: What is their age, gender, education, background, etc.?
I: Interest: Why would they be interested in looking at and reading your ePortfolio?

E: Environment: Where will your ePortfolio be viewed? What kind of computer with what capabilities might your audience members have?

N: Needs: What does your audience need? What can your ePortfolio offer to address those needs?

C: Customization: Knowing your audience, what specific needs or interests might you address in your ePortfolio?

E: Expectations: What will your audience expect to see and learn about in your ePortfolio?

CONCLUSION

Creating an ePortfolio is an opportunity for students to engage in understanding communication and integrative learning at a deeper level. They are making a product that has textual and visual components, and putting those things together to deliver a message is potentially richer than it could be if they only used the common textual forms used in the academy. This chapter provides strategies for helping students think about how they use all communication mediums and the impact they have on multiple audiences.

Creating the ePortfolio

This section is devoted to the *e* part of the ePortfolio, which is important if you are going to use ePortfolios in your courses, program, and institution. However, it is not the most important aspect of the process. The chapters in this section provide some basic ideas you should consider when thinking about how to introduce and use technology in helping students create ePortfolios.

Chapter 8 focuses on the structural aspects of the ePortfolio. What are the possible software or platforms? What kind of structure or architecture might you consider? What are privacy and control issues you might want to address? This chapter also provides a discussion and suggestions about how to think about introducing or expanding the use of ePortfolios outside individual classrooms.

Chapter 9 discusses teaching the technology used to create ePortfolios. We recommend creating a protocol to guide students in this process and provide a brief example using Google Sites.

As illustrated in Figure Part 3.1, this section addresses the technology side of the integrative learning ePortfolio framework.

Figure Part 3.1
Framework for Part Three

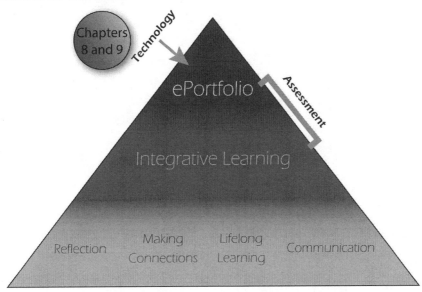

CHAPTER 8

Designing an ePortfolio System

Judy's story: Using technology to create ePortfolios is one of the most intimidating aspects of deciding to use ePortfolios in a class. I had it easy at first since I worked with an undergraduate peer mentor as a teaching partner, and making the ePortfolios took place in the mentor sessions in small computer labs. Mentors taught the technology using assignments we created together. I avoided dealing with the platform issues for years. Moving forward about 10 years, I now teach senior capstone classes on my own. I wanted to include ePortfolios but had no mentor or program assistance whatsoever. My first attempt was bumbling at best, and I put a lot of figuring out how things worked on my students. Candyce gave me a protocol for my students to use and helped me create a template. Still, it was touch and go. Thankfully, my students were very patient, and we worked together to create the first round of capstone ePortfolios in my classes. The next summer, the situation was improved by one important factor: I had finally created my own ePortfolio and had a much better understanding of the process and how to use the platform. I cannot recommend strongly enough that you make your own ePortfolio, and it is much more fun working with a partner or with a group of colleagues at your institution. Candyce and I worked with a group of colleagues called Out of Practice who decided together to walk the talk. We came to the conclusion that if we were so convinced that ePortfolios were transformational for students, we should be doing them ourselves. It was invaluable to have this group help us set deadlines and keep our feet to the fire to do the work to make our ePortfolios.

In this chapter, we use the integrative learning ePortfolio framework to think about implementing student ePortfolios in your classrooms and beyond. We then discuss how to choose a platform and include suggestions that might work for you. In Chapter 9 we give step-by-step instructions for creating an ePortfolio using Google Sites, the platform we use. We also discuss how a larger campus effort might begin and be implemented.

IMPLEMENTATION MODEL

The integrative learning ePortfolio framework is helpful in thinking about how to begin implementing ePortfolios in your classroom or at the department or institutional level. Figure 8.1 shows the steps in the implementation model. A fuller discussion follows.

1. *What is your goal for the ePortfolio?* We want to stress that you should not begin to think about using ePortfolios with the question of which platform to use. The most important thing is to determine how you want to use the ePortfolio, the practices, and the process. In Chapter 3 we discuss backward design and the need to start with the end in mind. In Chapter 7 we suggest that you encourage your students to think about the purpose and audience of their ePortfolios. In this chapter we encourage you to do something similar. Being clear about your learning outcomes and the practices you want to use will help you make an informed decision about how to implement the ePortfolio and what platform to use. After you have a good idea about what you want to do with your ePortfolios, then you can go through this model to decide which platform to use (see Step 5 in Figure 8.1).

2. *Assessment: Student, program, or institutional? How measured?* After clarifying your goal for the ePortfolio, consider how you will assess the ePortfolio. As we discuss in Chapter 10, at a minimum you will want to think about how you will grade the ePortfolio in your course, and you may need to think about assessment of the ePortfolio beyond your classroom for departmental or institutional purposes. Thinking about how you will assess the ePortfolio before you begin design or

Figure 8.1
Implementation Model

development helps you focus on what you want students to include in the ePortfolio. The underlying question is, How will you know your students have achieved the learning goals for the ePortfolio? Chapter 10 offers suggestions for using rubrics to determine this.

3. *What goes in the ePortfolio? Required elements? Student choice? Template?* Once you are clear about your goals for the ePortfolio and have thought about how you will measure students' achievement of those goals, you can then identify what should be in the ePortfolio. What are the required elements you will want to see in the ePortfolio? These will likely be directly tied to the assessment strategies you identified in Step 2. Decide how much free choice students will have in developing the content of the ePortfolio. Will they be required to include specific assignments to demonstrate their learning, or can they choose assignments they think best represent their learning? Can they include elements that go beyond the ePortfolio assignment including such things as work from other classes, links to favorite websites, and such? Do you need or want to provide students with a template, or is creating their own ePortfolio structure part of their learning?

4. *What can I do to support the development of the ePortfolio in the classroom and beyond?* Chapter 10 describes classroom strategies and activities that can support students in reaching your learning goals and building their ePortfolio. Again, these practices are the foundation of an integrative ePortfolio. Without determining and implementing these practices, students' ePortfolios will likely be disappointing.

5. *What is the platform I will use? How will students be supported?* Answering the questions in Steps 1–4 will help you get to the final step: deciding on a platform to use for your ePortfolio assignment. Without answering the preceding questions, it is impossible to know which features your platform needs to include. The next section discusses additional things you and your institution might consider in choosing a platform.

INDIVIDUAL FACULTY ADOPTION OF EPORTFOLIOS FOR CLASS OR PROJECT-BASED EPORTFOLIOS

A large range of software platforms to create ePortfolios is currently available. Some of them are free to use, and some can be purchased with learning management systems (LMSs) like Blackboard or Desire to Learn. Others are self-standing platforms that can work with certain other systems like LMSs, Google, Banner, or PeopleSoft. Each platform operates in specific ways; in fact, almost every day another ePortfolio platform or online strategy becomes available. So how do you decide what to use? The very structure of a system makes decisions for you. Every platform can do certain things. Most important, some systems are user friendly and some are not. Many platforms are very clunky and can frustrate you and your students, creating issues for class adoption. Others are structured more for assessment than for learning and reflection. Many faculty begin with a free software ePortfolio system, such as

- Google Sites (https://sites.google.com)
- Weebly (www.weebly.com)
- WordPress (http://wordpress.org)
- Wix (www.wix.com)

If your campus is a Google campus, you may also have free access to Digication, an application the institution can integrate with Google Apps for Education for campus use. (Alternatively, the software can be purchased directly from Digication at www.digication.com.)

Each of the platforms listed is for general website construction except WordPress, which is often used specifically to create blogs. Faculty who have chosen WordPress tell us that they can design attractive ePortfolios using it. Each platform has its pros and cons, but once you decide on one and begin using it, you will find it less challenging. Familiarity and practice helps a lot.

All these platforms contain instructions on how to build websites using their site. For more ideas or if you have questions, search the Internet for a multitude of answers. While the search results may not necessarily be the best or the most up-to-date, they can point you in the right direction. YouTube is also a good resource to create your own tutorials for your students to use. YouTube videos and other already developed tutorials using these platforms can easily be found on the web ready to adapt for your purposes.

Before you choose a platform, check with your technology office to see if it already supports one of the platforms. If it does, consider using that platform. Technology support at an institution can be extremely important. If your institution does not support any blog, website-building, or ePortfolio platforms, try to find a colleague who can help you become familiar with how to use the platform he or she uses. Form a support group with faculty who are interested in trying a blog, website, or ePortfolio in their classes. If you have an office of faculty development and instructional improvement or support, the staff there may know which faculty are already using technology in their classes and may even help set up the support group.

Students, however, are often your best resource. We suggest having at least one lab session for helping students get started on their ePortfolio. Usually, at least one student has had experience with the platform you have chosen or with one that is similar and readily volunteers to help others who are less technologically inclined. Once you have introduced ePortfolios in several of your classes, you can invite former students back to help your current students build the ePortfolio in the lab. Campus technology offices often provide lab assistants who can help in the computer labs while you are teaching the technology. The best way to become familiar with the technology is to create your own ePortfolio, as we said earlier. In the beginning, just keep it simple.

ISSUES OF PRIVACY AND CONTROL

Some of the first concerns faculty have when considering ePortfolios are those of privacy and control. Because ePortfolios are an individual's work—student, faculty, or staff—giving ultimate ownership to those individuals makes sense, educationally and ethically. What do privacy and control mean? Privacy means deciding who can see the ePortfolio, and control means who is allowed to have access to it and when. These issues become more important as institutions use ePortfolios for assessment, and as institutions and programs move toward using ePortfolios throughout an entire undergraduate or graduate experience. Giving an instructor or program the ability to access the ePortfolios at any particular time can be done during the system design and when creating settings for permissions to view or edit. For instance, architecture program staff let students know at the beginning that their work will be collected and used for program accreditation, which is required for the accreditation process. In a single class, instructors can set up the students' ePortfolios to give permission to the instructor to view them. The instructor can also require everyone in the class to have access to each other's ePortfolio. Students can simply include their classmates in their permissions settings when creating their sites.

In each platform, students can choose to

- publish to the world,
- restrict access to certain people, or
- keep it private.

We believe it is best to ask your students not to make their ePortfolios public in the beginning. Helping students understand what a digital identity is and how it can be helpful or not is part of the importance of using ePortfolios in the curriculum. Also, classroom-based ePortfolios do not necessarily belong on the web. They are to enhance and document learning in a particular situation, not for showcasing work, and should be shared only with the instructor and fellow classmates.

EPORTFOLIO STRUCTURE

To create the structure for your ePortfolios, recall your thinking on and planning how to integrate ePortfolios and integrative learning into your class (Chapter 3), and your assignments for making connections (Chapter 5). Often the ePortfolio assignment is the culminating class experience, and if this is the case, the structure of the ePortfolio should align with the course learning outcomes and offer students the opportunity to determine their achievement in those learning outcomes using your class activities and assignments as evidence. Students can create their ePortfolio shell at the beginning of the class and add activities and assignments in the appropriate places as the class progresses.

Here is a basic ePortfolio structure if you are using a culminating showcase ePortfolio in your class:

- A welcome page is the first page or place a reader lands on. It's an introduction to the ePortfolio and usually includes a photo or an image; short text; and navigation tools located on the left, top, or bottom of the page, or in more than one place, that are visible without scrolling and easy to navigate.
- A learning goals or outcomes page corresponds to each learning goal or outcome. Establishing a limit of 4–6 pages makes the process easier for students. Students can use these pages to
  - define the learning goal or outcome in their own language,
  - represent each goal or outcome page with an image or icon,
  - create links to work samples for each goal or outcome that demonstrate their capacity and ability in each goal or outcome area (work samples can serve for more than one goal), and
  - include reflections, which can be about the goal or outcome, what they have learned, but can also be about the work samples, explaining why they were chosen and why they represent their best work.
- A philosophy statement, a learner autobiography, or digital identity page whose content is determined by you as the instructor and what best fits with your course.
- A page containing a traditional résumé.

Exhibit 8.1 illustrates how to plan the ePortfolio for your course. You can also use this form as a handout.

CREATING TEMPLATES

Once you have decided on the structure of your ePortfolio, you can design a template for your students. A template, which is a shell with holding places for each part of the ePortfolio, makes it easy for less technologically experienced students to build an ePortfolio. Students simply fill in the spaces with their reflections, add photos or images, and link work in the appropriate areas. Students who want to and are more advanced technologically can build their own ePortfolios using the structure you have assigned. For instructions on creating a template using Google Sites, see Chapter 9.

MOVING TO INSTITUTION- OR PROGRAMWIDE USE

Once enough individual faculty members have found value in using ePortfolios and adopted integrative learning practices, the idea of a broader and longer term use of

Exhibit 8.1
Portfolio Structure

Structure	Description	When Activity Happens in Class	Activities/ Assignments That Demonstrate Learning	Reflections	Completed
Welcome page/ introduction to ePortfolio					
Learning goals/ outcomes					
1.					
2.					
3.					
4.					
5.					
6.					
Philosophy statement or "who am I?" statement/digital identity					
Résumé					
Contact information					

ePortfolios generally surfaces. It can also be that administrators of a major or program, such as general education, have adopted ePortfolios and believe an institution-level ePortfolio is a good idea as well.

The following are things you need to think about to find the best platform for your use:

- Decide how you want the ePortfolio process to work for students, faculty, and administrators. In other words, will it support learning, include reflective practice, and contain multiple drafts of work? Is it in accordance with the practices of faculty in the classroom to enhance student learning, the practices we have discussed in this book? If so, the platform needs to allow the practices and review process your institution decides to use.

- Look for a platform that is the easiest to use for those less technologically inclined.
- Take into account faculty concerns such as student privacy. Who will have access to student ePortfolios? How will access be controlled? How much control will students have over their ePortfolio?
- Will or could ePortfolios be used for faculty evaluation and the promotion and tenure process? How will that system work?
- Do you plan to use the ePortfolio for program or institutional assessment? If so, does the assessment process connect to teaching processes? Find out the assessment needs in terms of data, and make sure the platform fulfills those needs. However, make sure that student learning drives the design and decision making, not the assessment needs, an important, although secondary, concern. The ePortfolio can be used in assessment but that should not be the primary purpose.
- If there is an ePortfolio platform connected to an existing LMS, try it. If it does not accommodate the ways you plan to use ePortfolios, do not feel obligated to use it.
- What are the various costs of each platform and its support? It may be that the ePortfolio platform and its assessment function that is part of an existing LMS would be more expensive than a different platform. Many platforms will work with existing LMSs, and you should not feel that you have to use the ePortfolio platform that is part of the campus LMS.
- How will students and faculty take their ePortfolios with them when they leave the institution?

When choosing a platform,

- Do not leave it to the instructional technology (IT) people to make the decision alone and then inform faculty and staff after the fact. IT staff can and should be members of the decision-making group, and they will need to support the platform that is chosen, but they should not be the sole decision makers.
- Create a group to make the decision. This group should try out the platforms and even be involved in a pilot or pilots.
- Determine who your stakeholders are. The composition of the decision-making group should include teaching faculty who will use the platform and IT staff who will need to support the platform's use. It is a very good idea to include student representation or to get student input into the decision and the use of the platform as well. Representatives from upper administration should be brought in as advocates and be informed of the process since they will be funding the platform and implementation plan.

Figure 8.2
Choosing a Platform

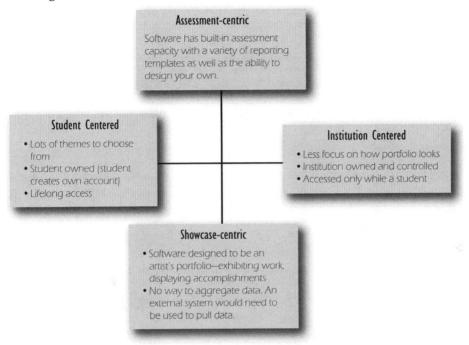

Note. From Garrison, W., and Ring. (2013). Walking the ePortfolio talk: Begin your ePortfolio in 4 hours. Workshop presented at the meeting of the Association of Authentic, Experiential and Evidence-Based Learning, July 2013, Boston, MA.

- Create an implementation plan for spreading the use of ePortfolios as part of the planning process. Cultivate the participation of informal faculty leaders to create a supportive culture.

Figure 8.2 shows a way to think about how you want to use your ePortfolios and helps you think about choosing a platform. The horizontal axis asks you to consider how student centered to institution centered you want the ePortfolios to be. The vertical axis concerns assessment use and showcase use. None of the uses negates the others. It is a matter of priorities and the way you design and use ePortfolios in the classroom. The free software platforms tend to fall in the student-centered, showcase-centric quadrant. The more commercial platforms fit more into the assessment-centric, institution-centered quadrant. A few platforms fall in the middle.

IMPLEMENTATION

As part of choosing a platform, try several and then choose one to pilot. Create an implementation team that includes enthusiastic faculty who may make up an entire department. Keep the pilot small because it is important to work out the bugs before a large group is encouraged to use ePortfolios. ePortfolio efforts have failed because of problems with implementation.

STRATEGIES

Create support materials as part of the implementation plan. Online tutorials, workshops, one-on-one consultations, or a combination of supports helps a positive, encouraging culture evolve. Many online tutorials can be used as guides. Try the tutorials on the platform's website and use them if they are well designed and guide the work easily.

Sharing the first ePortfolios can begin a conversation. Faculty respond well to seeing student work that is rich and represents a high standard. An ePortfolio showcase at the end of the year or term open to the department or campus can serve as a conversation impetus.

After an initial demonstration of what ePortfolios can look like and how they can be used, a strong strategy is faculty teaching faculty. Developing and supporting a community of practice (COP) or faculty learning community (LC) has worked well on several campuses. Often these COPs or LCs are supported by centers for teaching and learning on campuses. With a small amount of funding for stipends or even just to serve cookies, faculty can be invited to join LCs. The following describes LCs and how they work:

- LCs are led by experienced faculty who plan a term or year of meetings and activities to help other faculty envision, design, and implement ePortfolios for their classes. Staff from IT can help as well.
- Groups commit to meeting monthly or to some other regular schedule.
- The leader selects reading material, such as the following, that participants use to prepare for each session:
  - This book as well as many articles and other books on ePortfolios are possibilities.
  - Existing materials can help faculty understand what ePortfolios can do can and how they can be used. See the Association of American Colleges and Universities' (AAC&U) website (www.aacu.org/programs/index.cfm)

for resources and descriptions of projects regarding liberal education that may be helpful as you make a case for using ePortfolios for instruction and assessment. The Liberal Education and America's Promise (LEAP) project may be especially useful in helping leaders on your campus understand the need for promoting integrative learning in the academy (see www.aacu.org/leap/index.cfm). Studies found on this website on what employers value, how people are now applying for jobs online and using ePortfolios, and examples of successful use of ePortfolios helps make the case for adopting ePortfolios.

- Leaders can also use ePortfolios, integrative learning demonstration websites, and work by their own colleagues.

- It is important to include some type of final product as part of a commitment to this group, such as a revised syllabus using integrative learning practices and assignments and ePortfolios. Sessions can be devoted to creating these materials and support for first-time application of the new methodologies.

Try to avoid top-down efforts. Faculty and student interest supported by the administration works very well. If this is a campuswide effort, send teams to ePortfolio conferences such as the annual conference for the Association for Authentic, Experiential and Evidence-Based Learning or AAC&U's ePortfolio symposium at its annual meeting. If you have the budget, you can host informational meetings inviting some ePortfolio experts to your campus.

Whatever process you choose, plenty of help is available. For example, contact someone at Electronic Portfolio Action and Communication at http://epac.pbworks.com for support.

EPORTFOLIOS FOR FACULTY

Institutions are also adopting electronic promotion and tenure portfolios for faculty. Faculty ePortfolios can be more attractive than paper files, easier to update and store, and easier to share and evaluate. Before you decide to create an ePortfolio for your evaluation, make sure your department chair and upper administration are willing to accept it. Many faculty are also creating professional ePortfolios to enhance their practice and to share their work in a larger arena. Some faculty have created private ePortfolios to keep track of their personal reflections on teaching and on their scholarship. As with student ePortfolios, you decide who has permission to view your ePortfolio or parts of it.

CONCLUSION

The *e* part of the ePortfolio is important, but it is not the most important. Thinking through the purpose of your ePortfolio project will help you make good decisions about the platform you want to use and how you want to implement the project. This chapter discusses strategies for adding the ePortfolio to your course and your institution.

Chapter 9

Making an ePortfolio Using Free Web-Based Software

*Judy and Candyce's story: Candy*ce led the mentor program in University Studies, while Judy was director of the program. In University Studies, peer mentors worked with the faculty who taught Freshman Inquiry, and graduate mentors worked with faculty teaching Sophomore Inquiry courses. As director of mentor programs, Candyce had contact with all the new and continuing mentors and designed the training they undertook each spring term prior to their becoming mentors the following fall. The mentors became an invaluable resource for the program. Their inventiveness, dedication to the goals of the program, and the knowledge they brought from their majors, previous experience, and understanding of technology helped everyone. They made every good idea better. When Candyce decided they needed a resource site, the mentors created a website better than anything we had envisioned. When we had questions about technology, what to use and how to use it, the mentors had strong perspectives. They were students too and could give us a student perspective on how the program was or could work better. We asked two mentors to participate on the first ePortfolio system design committee. They were the first to say that the technology or platform is not the most important factor. They told us that the time it took to teach the technology that students would probably never use again would be better spent on the more substantial goals of the program. They advised us to find the easiest platform we could and spend the classroom time on reflection rather than on teaching technology. It was a key lesson in our development of the ePortfolio.

While we know that technology should not be the driver when teaching a student how to create an ePortfolio, we also recognize that you will need to teach some kind of software at some point. We recommend that you develop a simple protocol you can use to teach the basics in a lab that students can then take to guide them as they continue to work on their ePortfolios. In Exhibit 9.1, we provide a sample protocol for building an ePortfolio and instructions for creating and saving a template for your students. This protocol or tutorial is for Google Sites, one of the applications available with a Google account. Whether you choose to use Google Sites or another platform, we hope this protocol will at a minimum help you see what students need to get started to learn the technology.

It is important to give your students an easy-to-follow, clear set of instructions to use to create their first ePortfolios. We also caution you to check your instructions before every term. The platforms change often, and when this happens instructions need tweaking. Also, colors and instructions for a specific platform can vary depending on your browser (especially true of Google Sites). Make sure your students understand there could be minor variations on their computers to avoid confusion.

GOOGLE SITES

Google Sites was adopted by University Studies at PSU when we became a Google campus. Most faculty who use ePortfolios at the institution now use Google Sites because University Studies adopted it.

A good thing about Google Sites is that Google provides written online tutorials for it. You can also find YouTube videos that show you how to create your Google Sites ePortfolio. Some find Google Sites difficult to learn and nonintuitive, but with minimal instruction and support, we have found it works well for us. And, it is free. But make sure you check before telling your students about it in case Google has changed its policies.

Exhibit 9.1
Google Sites Protocol

Step-by-Step Instructions for Starting Your ePortfolio Using Google Sites

1. Go to accounts.google.com and create a Google account if you don't have one already.
2. Navigate to Google Sites (sites.google.com).
3. Click the "Create" button on the left-hand side of the screen.
4. The first thing you will see is the "select a template to use" area. If your professor has created a template for you to use, you can find it under the "Browse gallery for more" area. You can also choose "Blank Template."
5. Enter your site name in the "Name Your Site" box. The URL where it will be located (e.g., sites.google.com/site/yoursite) will be created for you. The name and URL you choose cannot be changed after you create your site, or used again if the site is deleted. Consider using your name for the name on your URL. This is the most professional way to name your site. Use your middle initial if your name is already taken. Avoid hyphens or numbers in your URL.

---

6. Pick a design theme for your site—there are several variations to choose from. You can try them out and see which fits the digital identity you want to create. This option follows the "Name your site" area, lower on the first screen. You also have the option of adding a site description.

7. Complete the CAPTCHA (transcribe the wavy characters you see in the image presented), and click the "Create" button at the top of the screen. When it is created, you will be taken to your new site. This may take a few moments.

8. When your site comes up, you will see three icons on the top right of the screen: a pencil, a page with a corner turned down and a plus on it, and a gear.

9. Click the gear-shaped icon at the top of the screen and select "Sharing and Permissions" from the drop-down menu. Select one of the sharing options: "Public on the web," "Anyone with the link," or "Specific people." Your professor may have already told you which option to choose. It is best to wait to publish to the world until you are ready to show your ePortfolio.

10. Personalize your landing page by clicking on the pencil icon. Once you click the pencil, the editing toolbar will come up and you can edit the title, text, and images on the page. You can insert images by clicking "Insert" in the toolbar and selecting the image file from your computer. Once you have inserted an image, you can change the size by clicking on the image and then clicking S, M, or L. You have options for wrapping the text as well. Make sure you click "Save" every time you add or change anything on your page.

11. Now that you've created your site, you can create a new page by clicking the "New page" button, the page-shaped icon. Name the page and select the template you want to use: webpage, announcement, file cabinet, or list. Generally, you will want a webpage. After you have selected where you want to locate the page, click "Create" at the top of the screen. These pages will become your navigation system. Each page you want to appear on the left, place below your home page. You can add pages under those main pages but the titles will not appear on your home page.

12. To change your permissions or delete the entire site, click the gear icon and select "Manage site."

TEMPLATES

Another successful strategy is to create templates for your students' ePortfolios, which are shells students can fill in with their text. They do not need to design the site; they simply fill in the assigned reflections, learning goals, and definitions and attach work samples. Offering a template to students who are not comfortable with technology is a big step in helping them create an ePortfolio and also gain confidence using technology.

To create a template, follow the directions for creating an ePortfolio in Exhibit 9.1, but in each area, such as the introduction page, let your students know the kind of information you want them to supply for each section. For instance, in the text area on the home page your instruction could be, "Write a brief description of yourself and your educational goals in this space." Create a page for each learning goal for your course; you can add more pages to give your students places for their own learning goals as well. Then do the following:

1. Click the gear icon at the top of the screen, then choose "Manage site."
2. Click "General" on the left side of the page, scroll down, and click "Publish this site as a template."
3. A form will appear in which you can name your template and add a description of what it might be used to achieve. You also have the option of placing your template in up to two categories (if available); to do this, choose a category from each of the "Select a Category" lists.
4. Click "Submit." The template appears in the gallery with the name and description you gave it.

For many faculty and students, tools such as a protocol or clear and well-written instructions make creating an ePortfolio possible. When students have completed the ePortfolio, they feel accomplished and confident, and you have a clear record of what your students have gained in your courses.

CONCLUSION

Although the *e* is not the most important part of the ePortfolio process, it is a necessary one. This chapter provides a sample protocol for using Google Sites to guide your students in creating a basic ePortfolio. We also discuss and give instructions for creating a template for your students. A template can make the technical part of the ePortfolio even easier for students. Again, students' major energy should be directed at developing their reflections and contents of the ePortfolio; the technology part should not overshadow this effort.

PART FOUR

At the End

The final section of this book would not be complete without a discussion about what typically happens when an ePortfolio is complete: assessment.

Chapter 10 focuses on individual student assessment and program and institutional assessment. It discusses the use of rubrics for assessment and provides several examples to help you get started in using rubrics in your work. A description of how you can use ePortfolio assessment in your grading is provided as well as a process of using rubrics for program assessment.

Chapter 11 contains some closing thoughts.

As shown in Figure Part 4.1, this section addresses assessment of the integrative learning ePortfolio framework.

Figure Part 4.1
Framework for Part Four

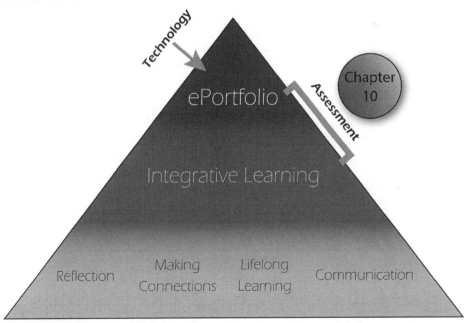

CHAPTER 10

Assessment of ePortfolios

Using Rubrics to Assess

Judy's story: When I was first introduced to assessment, I thought, finally, a way to really know what my students are actually getting from my classes. We all have assumptions about what students learn in our classes, but those assumptions are most often untested. Assessment provides ways to ask questions about those assumptions and find out how reliable they were. However, I found that my colleagues did not always agree with my positive view. Many faculty see assessment as very threatening. As we worked our way through the faculty teaching in University Studies, we found that asking them to identify a question they had about their teaching helped them see the benefits that assessment could bring. I remember one faculty member in particular who said his class was fine, that he had students who were just not prepared for his material. Some of his students were able to understand the concepts he was teaching, but some of them were not ready for his class. So we did a short survey about preparation, and we found that the students he had identified as being prepared had already taken a similar class, and the material was not new to them. That's why they were getting it. It wasn't because they were smarter overall; it was because they were familiar with the course content while the other students were new to it. It was an eye-opening moment for him, and he never thought about his students or taught that class in the same way.

In this chapter we discuss the broader context of accountability and its relation to assessment using ePortfolios. We move on to ways to use ePortfolios for student grading and how to do ePortfolio assessment, and we include strategies, processes, and tools.

THE CONTEXT OF ACCOUNTABILITY

Higher education is under great pressure today to demonstrate student learning and show the value that education adds to a student's life. The Association of American Colleges and Universities (AAC&U) has been leading the way through its research and programs. Its work has helped determine and express what society at large and

131

employers expect from college graduates. Hart Research Associates (2013) provides data and arguments showing that a liberal education and the abilities that kind of education develops match the expectations of parents, employers, and legislators.

At this point, higher education has staved off a common high-stakes, multiple-choice exit exam. However, government officials, even at the highest level, seem to want to reduce higher education to the lowest common denominator, degree attainment. As we know degree attainment does not necessarily equal learning. Without ways to measure the quality of learning, degree attainment is an empty promise. The types of assessments suggested by government do not result in data that help students or teachers improve educational outcomes. Student success on tests and measures has more to do with the individual student's family's economic level and his or her ability to take tests well than a meaningful understanding of what students know and are able to do after their education. ePortfolios offer a richer way to assess student learning and can also answer the questions faculty members have about learning in their courses as well as give institutions data that can demonstrate institutional success.

Carol Geary Schneider (2009), president of AAC&U, says this about ePortfolios:

> Policy leaders have asked for transparency about student performance. In response, we must point out that ill-focused tests can be neither transparent nor informative about what a student has accomplished, over time, on a range of learning outcomes that are important to our economy, our democracy, and his or her own hopes for the future.
>
> What then should we recommend? Educators around the country are pointing to an accountability strategy that can provide, simultaneously, a framework for raising student achievement, evidence of progress over time, and transparency about the extent to which students are achieving what AAC&U's LEAP initiative calls "essential learning outcomes."
>
> The strategy—well attuned to the technologies of our time—uses e-portfolios, or what we might call "supplemental transcripts." Already adopted by institutions as diverse as the University of Michigan, LaGuardia Community College, Hampshire, and Carleton and in development at many others, e-portfolios enable us to see what a student is working on over time, to discern an emerging sense of purpose and direction, and to review samples of writing, research projects, and creative work as well as progress in integrating learning across multiple levels of schooling and multiple areas of study and experience. An e-portfolio also opens windows into a student's field-based assignments by creating opportunities to present supervisor evaluations or even videos showing real-world performance. They can be sampled, using rubrics, for external reporting. (p. 1)

While we believe student ePortfolios should always have a primary focus on learning, they also provide an important strategy for assessing learning using authentic student work. The institutions most recognized for using ePortfolios for institutional or program-level assessment are Alverno College, Clemson University, Portland State University (PSU), LaGuardia Community College, and Spelman College. Each institution has developed a process for evaluating the ePortfolio that generally looks at the first-year curriculum or at general education. Clemson uses ePortfolios to assess its undergraduate general education outcomes. Each institution has developed its own process for assessing ePortfolios.

THE ASSESSMENT PROCESS: RUBRICS

The most common strategy for evaluating ePortfolios is rubrics. Many faculty have adopted rubrics for grading individual assignments, including an ePortfolio, to create a more transparent and equitable way of evaluation. Rubrics can also be used to assess program or institutional-level outcomes. As we discuss in previous chapters, we are fortunate to have VALUES (AAC&U, n.d.) rubrics that provide a means for assessing liberal learning outcomes at an institution or can provide a starting point for the development of institutionally specific rubrics.

According to Andrade (n.d.),

> A rubric is a scoring tool that lists the criteria for a piece of work, or "what counts" (for example, purpose, organization, details, voice and mechanics are often what count in a piece of writing); it also articulates gradations of quality for each criterion, from excellent to poor. (para. 3)

Stevens and Levi (2005) suggest that using rubrics aids in giving students timely feedback, helping students learn how to use that feedback, encouraging critical thinking about the work, and enhancing communication between the student and others who help students with their work. Beyond the grading, rubrics also help faculty refine their teaching and, perhaps most important, level the playing field for students.

> Rubrics offer a way for us to pinpoint problems in communication and deal with them until we are sure that our students are actually speaking the same language we are. Then we can communicate our expectations in ways that go beyond merely knowing the content of the class, especially if the rubrics are discussed or even constructed in class. (Stevens & Levi, 2005, p. 27)

Most faculty have rubrics in mind; they have some criteria that form the basis for their grading. Creating a rubric means bringing those criteria out of their heads and putting them on paper. Making the criteria visible makes grading easier and faster and helps students achieve the level of work expected. "Rubrics divide an assignment into its component parts and provide a detailed description of what constitutes acceptable or unacceptable levels of performance for each of those parts" (Stevens & Levi, 2005, p. 3).

An almost limitless number of rubrics can be found online for a wide variety of assignments and disciplines. Blank forms are available as well, and you can use the examples you find to create your own rubrics for your specific assignments and courses. It can also be helpful to ask your class to develop the rubric by discussing what would be considered good work for an assignment and then create the rubric using the categories and criteria agreed upon by the class. This exercise helps students understand from the ground up what your expectations are, why you are assigning the work, and what you hope the students achieve by doing the work. By engaging in collaborative rubric design, students become more internally motivated to do the work, and this kind of partnership with students helps them develop autonomy in their learning.

Assessment of ePortfolios using rubrics can happen at the individual student level in your course but can also be used for program or institutional assessment. First, we discuss individual student assessment and then move to program or institutional assessment.

USING RUBRICS IN YOUR COURSES

We recommend trying rubrics for one assignment first. Look online or ask a colleague for some sample rubrics that apply to your field or even your assignment. You can adopt a rubric you find or use it as a foundation for creating your own. A rubric basically lists the categories you will be looking at to evaluate the work and the levels of attainment and their corresponding scores. We begin with an example of a rubric for writing because it is a common practice that faculty value and crosses almost all fields. We'll follow with other examples of rubrics you could adapt for use in your own courses, one on reflective practice and one used to evaluate an ePortfolio holistically.

In Exhibit 10.1 the levels of quality are across the top of the rubric. The levels are: simple, no/limited proficiency, some proficiency, proficiency, and high proficiency. The first column contains the criteria or categories that will be evaluated in the assignment or work. For this rubric, they are originality and clarity in thesis/focus, organization, ideas and details in support/reasoning, and use of documentation sources. You assign points to each category and level of proficiency. Score the student's paper awarding the appropriate points for each criterion, add the points, and you have the student's score. For example, if the paper is worth 25 points, you can give up to 5 points for each criterion. Each level in that criterion would receive 0 to 2 points, adding up to the total of 5. The number of points you give to each criterion and level (e.g., 1, 3, 5) tells the student how much importance you give to each criterion.

Assessing Reflective Practice

Reflective practice is part of all ePortfolio systems. The student reflections are often used to assess their writing and critical thinking; however, institutions are beginning to see the value in assessing the reflective practice itself. Using the journal rubric in Exhibit 10.2, students can see the level of expectation for their journals and understand what it takes to engage in meaningful reflective practice.

Exhibit 10.1
Rubric to Score Writing

Quality Criteria	No/Limited Proficiency	Some Proficiency	Proficiency	High Proficiency	(Rating)
1. Thesis/focus: (a) Originality	Thesis is missing.	Thesis may be obvious or unimaginative.	Thesis is somewhat original.	Develops fresh insight that challenges the reader's thinking.	
2. Thesis/focus: (b) Clarity	Reader cannot determine thesis and purpose or thesis has no relation to the writing task.	Thesis and purpose are somewhat vague OR only loosely related to the writing task.	Thesis and purpose are fairly clear and match the writing task.	Thesis and purpose are clear to the reader; closely match the writing task.	
3. Organization	Unclear organization or organizational plan is inappropriate to thesis. No transitions.	Some signs of logical organization. May have abrupt or illogical shifts and ineffective flow of ideas.	Organization supports thesis and purpose. Transitions are mostly appropriate. Sequence of ideas could be improved.	Fully and imaginatively supports thesis and purpose. Sequence of ideas is effective. Transitions are effective.	
4. Support/ reasoning (a) Ideas (b) Details	Offers simplistic, undeveloped, or cryptic support for the ideas. Inappropriate or off-topic generalizations, faulty assumptions, errors of fact.	Offers somewhat obvious support that may be too broad. Details are too general, not interpreted, irrelevant to thesis, or inappropriately repetitive.	Offers solid but less original reasoning. Assumptions are not always recognized or made explicit. Contains some appropriate details or examples.	Substantial, logical, and concrete development of ideas. Assumptions are made explicit. Details are germane, original, and convincingly interpreted.	

(Continues)

Exhibit 10.1
Rubric to Score Writing (Continued)

Quality Criteria	No/Limited Proficiency	Some Proficiency	Proficiency	High Proficiency	(Rating)
5. Use of sources/documentation	Neglects important sources. Overuse of quotations or paraphrase to substitute writer's own ideas. (Possibly uses source material without acknowledgment)	Uses relevant sources but lacks in variety of sources and/or the skillful combination of sources. Quotations and paraphrases may be too long and/ or inconsistently referenced.	Uses sources to support, extend, and inform, but not substitute writer's own development of idea. Doesn't overuse quotes, but may not always conform to required style manual.	Uses sources to support, extend, and inform, but not substitute writer's own development of idea. Combines material from a variety of sources, including personal observation, scientific data, authoritative testimony. Doesn't overuse quotes.	

Note. From "Rubric to Score Writing," by B. E. Walvoord, 2013, South Bend, IN: University of Notre Dame. www.azwestern.edu/learning_services/instruction/center_teaching_effect/resources/downloads/Writing%20Rubric%20Barbara%20Wal-voord.pdf. Copyright 2013 by B. E. Walvoord. Reprinted with permission.

Exhibit 10.2
Sample Scoring Rubric for a Student Journal

Levels	Criteria
Reflective practitioner	Clarity: The language is clear and expressive. The reader can create a mental picture of the situation being described. Abstract concepts are explained accurately. Explanation of concepts makes sense to an uninformed reader.
	Relevance: The learning experience being reflected upon is relevant and meaningful to student and course learning goals.
	Analysis: The reflection moves beyond simple description of the experience to an analysis of how the experience contributed to student understanding of self, others, and/or course concepts. Analysis has both breadth (incorporation of multiple perspectives) and depth (premises and claims supported by evidence).
	Interconnections: The reflection demonstrates connections between the experience and material from other courses, past experience, and/or personal goals.
	Self-criticism: The reflection demonstrates ability of the student to question his or her own biases, stereotypes, preconceptions, and/or assumptions and define new modes of thinking as a result.
Aware practitioner	Clarity: Minor, infrequent lapses in clarity and accuracy.
	Relevance: The learning experience being reflected upon is relevant and meaningful to student and course learning goals.
	Analysis: The reflection demonstrates student attempts to analyze the experience but analysis lacks depth and breadth.
	Interconnections: The reflection demonstrates connections between the experience and material from other courses, past experience, and/or personal goals.
	Self-criticism: The reflection demonstrates ability of the student to question his or her own biases, stereotypes, and preconceptions.

(Continues)

Exhibit 10.2
Sample Scoring Rubric for a Student Journal (*Continued*)

Levels	Criteria
Reflection novice	Clarity: There are frequent lapses in clarity and accuracy.
	Relevance: Student makes attempts to demonstrate relevance, but the relevance is unclear to the reader.
	Analysis: Student makes attempts at applying the learning experience to understanding of self, others, and/or course concepts but fails to demonstrate depth and breadth of analysis.
	Interconnections: There is little to no attempt to demonstrate connections between the learning experience and previous other personal and/or learning experiences.
	Self-criticism: There is some attempt at self-criticism, but the self-reflection fails to demonstrate a new awareness of personal biases, etc.
Unacceptable	Clarity: Language is unclear and confusing throughout. Concepts are either not discussed or are presented inaccurately.
	Relevance: Most of the reflection is irrelevant to student and/or course learning goals.
	Analysis: Reflection does not move beyond description of the learning experience(s).
	Interconnection: No attempt to demonstrate connections to previous learning or experience.
	Self-criticism: No attempt at self-criticism.

Note. From "Using Reflection for Assessment," by S. Jones, n.d., http://studentlife.uiowa.edu/assets/Using-Reflection-for-Assessment.pdf. Copyright 2013 by S. Jones. Adapted with permission.

Holistic ePortfolio Assessment

Holistic ePortfolio assessment means looking at the construction, design, and work as a complete artifact. When the work, the reflections, and the navigation of the ePortfolio all contribute to the assessment, holistic ePortfolio rubrics are used. Most often the individual student work samples are part of the holistic assessment and meet general ePortfolio criteria for that work.

The rubric in Exhibit 10.3 illustrates the difference between the holistic rubric and rubrics for specific learning outcomes. The holistic rubric evaluates the ePortfolio as an entire piece of work and includes the categories that describe it, such as selection

Exhibit 10.3
Holistic ePortfolio Rubric

Criteria	Unsatisfactory—0%	Limited—80%	Proficient—90%	Exemplary—100%	Rating
Selection of Artifacts Weight for this criterion: 40% of total score	The artifacts and work samples do not relate to the purpose of the ePortfolio.	Some of the artifacts and work samples are related to the purpose of the ePortfolio.	Most artifacts and work samples are related to the purpose of the ePortfolio.	All artifacts and work samples are clearly and directly related to the purpose of the ePortfolio. A wide variety of artifacts is included.	
	No artifacts are accompanied by a caption that clearly explains the importance of the item including title, author, and date.	Some of the artifacts are accompanied by a caption that clearly explains the importance of the item including title, author, and date.	Most of the artifacts are accompanied by a caption that clearly explains the importance of the item work including title, author, and date.	All artifacts are accompanied by a caption that clearly explains the importance of the item including title, author, and date.	
Reflection/ Critique Weight for this criterion: 30% of total score	The reflections do not describe growth or include goals for continued learning.	A few of the reflections describe growth and include goals for continued learning.	Most of the reflections describe growth and include goals for continued learning.	All reflections clearly describe growth, achievement, accomplishments, and include goals for continued learning (long and short term).	
	The reflections do not illustrate the ability to effectively critique work or provide suggestions for constructive practical alternatives.	A few reflections illustrate the ability to effectively critique work and provide suggestions for constructive practical alternatives.	Most of the reflections illustrate the ability to effectively critique work and provide suggestions for constructive practical alternatives.	All reflections illustrate the ability to effectively critique work and provide suggestions for constructive practical alternatives.	

(Continues)

Exhibit 10.3
Holistic ePortfolio Rubric (*Continued*)

Criteria	Unsatisfactory—0%	Limited—80%	Proficient—90%	Exemplary—100%	Rating
Use of Multimedia Weight for this criterion: 10% of total score	The graphic elements or multimedia do not contribute to understanding concepts, ideas and relationships. The inappropriate use of multimedia detracts from the content.	Some of the graphic elements and multimedia do not contribute to understanding concepts, ideas, and relationships.	Most of the graphic elements and multimedia contribute to understanding concepts, ideas and relationships, enhance the written material and create interest.	All of the photographs, concept maps, spreadsheets, graphics, audio, and/or video files effectively enhance understanding of concepts, ideas and relationships, create interest, and are appropriate for the chosen purpose.	
	The graphics do not include alternate text in web-based portfolios.	Some of the graphics include alternate text in web-based portfolios.	Most of the graphics include alternate text in web-based portfolios.	Accessibility requirements using alternate text for graphics are included in web-based portfolios.	
	Audio and/or video artifacts are not edited or exhibit inconsistent clarity or sound (too loud/too soft/garbled).	A few of the audio and/or video artifacts are edited with inconsistent clarity or sound (too loud/too soft/garbled).	Most of the audio and/or video artifacts are edited with proper voice projection, appropriate language, and clear delivery.	All audio and/or video artifacts are edited with proper voice projection, appropriate language, and clear delivery.	
Citations Weight for this criterion: 5% of total score	No images, media, or text created by others are cited with accurate, properly formatted citations.	Some of the images, media, or text created by others are not cited with accurate, properly formatted citations.	Most images, media, or text elements created by others are cited with accurate, properly formatted citations.	All images, media, and text follow copyright guidelines with accurate citations. All content throughout the ePortfolio displays the appropriate copyright permissions.	

Navigation Weight for this criterion: 5% of total score	The navigation links are confusing, and it is difficult to locate artifacts and move to related pages or a different section. There are significant problems with pages connecting to preceding pages or the table of contents. Many of the external links do not connect to the appropriate website or file.	The navigation links are somewhat confusing, and it is often unclear how to locate an artifact or move to related pages or a different section. Some of the pages connect to the table of contents, but in other places the links do not connect to preceding pages or to the table of contents. Some of the external links do not connect to the appropriate website or file.	The navigation links generally function well, but it is not always clear how to locate an artifact or move to related pages or different section. Most of the pages connect to the table of contents. Most of the external links connect to the appropriate website or file.	The navigation links are intuitive. The various parts of the portfolio are labeled, clearly organized, and allow the reader to easily locate an artifact and move to related pages or a different section. All pages connect to the table of contents, and all external links connect to the appropriate website or file.
Layout and Readability Weight for this criterion: 5% of total score	The ePortfolio is difficult to read due to inappropriate use of fonts, type size for headings, sub-headings, and text and font styles (italic, bold, underline). Many formatting tools are under or over-utilized and decrease the readers' accessibility to the content.	The ePortfolio is often difficult to read due to inappropriate use of fonts and type size for headings, sub-headings, and text or inconsistent use of font styles (italic, bold, underline). Some formatting tools are under or over-utilized and decrease the readers' accessibility to the content.	The ePortfolio is generally easy to read.	The ePortfolio is easy to read.

(Continues)

Exhibit 10.3
Holistic ePortfolio Rubric (Continued)

Criteria	Unsatisfactory—0%	Limited—80%	Proficient—90%	Exemplary—100%	Rating
	Color of background, fonts, and links decreases the readability of the text, is distracting and used inconsistently throughout the ePortfolio.	Color of background, fonts, and links decreases the readability of the text, is distracting and used inconsistently in some places throughout the ePortfolio.	Color, background, font styles, and type size for headings, sub-headings and text are generally used consistently throughout the ePortfolio.	Color, background, font styles (italic, bold, underline) and type size for headings, sub-headings and text are used consistently and enhance the readability throughout the ePortfolio.	
	Horizontal and vertical white space alignment is used inappropriately, and the content appears disorganized and cluttered.	Horizontal and vertical white space alignment is sometimes used inappropriately to organize content.	Horizontal and vertical white space alignment is generally used appropriately to organize content.	Horizontal and vertical white space alignment is used appropriately to organize content.	
Quality of Writing and Proofreading Weight for this criterion: 5% of total score	There are numerous grammatical, spelling, or punctuation errors. The style of writing does not facilitate effective communication and requires major editing and revision.	The writing includes some grammatical, spelling, or punctuation errors that distract the reader and requires some editing and revision.	The writing is largely free of grammatical, spelling, or punctuation errors. The style of writing generally facilitates communication and minor editing is required.	The writing is free of grammatical, spelling, or punctuation errors. The style of writing facilitates communication and no editing is required.	
				TOTAL	

Note. From "EPortfolio (Digital Portfolio) Rubric," by J. M. Vandervelde, 2012, https://www2.uwstout.edu/content/profdev/rubrics/eportfolio rubric.html. Copyright 2012 by J. M. Vandervelde. Reprinted with permission.

of artifacts, reflection/critique, use of multimedia, citations, navigation, layout and readability, and quality of writing and proofreading. The rubric weights each category as well.

Assessment as Individual Grading

At this point in the development of ePortfolios, individual student evaluation is by far the primary use. Virtually all ePortfolios are used as part of the grading scheme in a course. In grading, instructional faculty develop the curriculum for their courses and are responsible for evaluating the student work required for the course. Grading takes individual student progress into consideration. Faculty may be concerned about using ePortfolios because they can perceive it to be difficult to grade all the work at the end of the term or year. The following are ways to manage this issue depending on the situation:

- The ePortfolio alone is required for a course grade, but the work included in the ePortfolio has already been graded as part of the course. In this case, the completed ePortfolio gives the student course credit. Students must turn in the ePortfolio in order to complete the course and receive course credit.
- Students compile ePortfolios and will have received feedback and grades on their work. At the end of the term or course, all faculty teaching sections of the course exchange student ePortfolios and grade the work in them using a programwide rubric. This evaluation can result in a course grade and can serve as program-level assessment of a core course in a program. This strategy is common in writing programs.
- The ePortfolio is evaluated using a holistic scoring rubric. In this way, the ePortfolio itself rather than individual pieces of work are evaluated for a course grade (see Exhibit 10.3).

Assessment of Program or Institutional Learning Outcomes

For assessment of programs or institutions, we are looking for program- or institutional-level data. Assessment data can show how the curriculum in a program is working but does not address individual student achievement or even individual faculty evaluation. Often, faculty fear assessment as a means for the administration to target or critique their teaching. It is important to make the use of assessment data and the process for gathering it as transparent as possible and to make it part of program planning and curriculum development. Assessment should not be a top-down endeavor but a collaborative activity that can further program and institutional goals. The following are ways to use ePortfolios for assessment:

- Students tag work in their ePortfolios and submit it under specific learning outcomes for evaluation. For example, at Clemson, trained student peer evaluators do the first-level evaluation: The work meets the required level or it does not. In this way, students have the opportunity to redo work before submitting the ePortfolios before graduation. At the end of the year, faculty use campuswide rubrics to score the students' work in seven learning outcomes for graduation.

- Students design their ePortfolios based on program learning outcomes and determine where to place work they believe demonstrates their learning in those specific outcomes. Students reflect on the meaning of the outcomes, why they chose the specific work they did, and how their learning has developed over the course. This process is used by PSU's first-year course, Freshman Inquiry. At the end of each year, groups of faculty, staff, and student mentors assess the student work according to particular outcomes, scoring them using programwide rubrics. The Freshman Inquiry teaching teams receive their data and can revise their curriculum making use of that data.

- Students place work in the specified area of the ePortfolio for certain learning outcomes at the levels of the program they are in, such as a 100-, 200-, 300- or 400 level course. Each course has a specific key assignment for each learning outcome. Each course states what learning outcomes at what level students will be assigned. Faculty evaluate the work that has been done in that class for the course grades using a rubric developed by the faculty for major outcomes and for general education outcomes. The grades, then, are the institutional means of assessing learning. This system is used at Alverno.

ASSESSMENT PROCESSES

A basic ePortfolio process is used by PSU's University Studies program for its Freshman Inquiry ePortfolios and could be easily adapted at your institution for program-level ePortfolio assessment. University Studies assesses one learning outcome per day. The program has four learning outcomes but assesses separately the two categories of writing and quantitative reasoning under the communication goal. The critical thinking rubric is shown in Exhibit 10.4. All the goals, their definitions, and rubrics for assessment are available at www.pdx.edu/university-studies-goals. The following is the process used by University Studies:

1. Students create ePortfolios as part of the curriculum. The ePortfolios to be assessed at the end of the year after grades have been submitted are randomly selected. A random number generator can be used based on course rosters. Faculty are given the numbers or names of the ePortfolios to send in for assessment. At least 25% of the enrollment in Freshman Inquiry needs to be assessed for enough significant data to draw conclusions. ePortfolio URLs can be used or CDs or flash drives of the ePortfolio can be submitted if the institution or program does not have an ePortfolio system in place.

2. The number of learning outcomes to be assessed is determined as part of the assessment planning. A different outcome is assessed each day. The program staff calls for volunteers several weeks prior to the scheduled assessment days. Faculty, staff, graduate students, and undergraduate student mentors volunteer to do the evaluation. Most institutions pay per day and host a meal as part of the assessment activity since the assessment usually takes place after the academic year.

3. Each day begins with a calibration of the rubric that will be used that day.

   a. Calibration

      i. All the evaluators read the same work sample.

      ii. When everyone has read and scored the work, they share their scores, which the leader writes on a board or paper.

      iii. Those who score higher or lower than the majority are asked to share their reasoning.

      iv. The evaluators discuss the scoring until a consensus becomes clear.

      v. It is important to point out that this is not the time to critique the rubric. If discussion moves in that direction, the whole assessment day can fall apart. Instead, ask each evaluator to write any comments on the rubrics or process on a separate sheet of paper to be handed in at the end of the day.

      vi. At the end of the calibration activity, the actual ePortfolio assessment begins.

4. Each work sample should be read by at least two evaluators. The evaluators hand in their scores or log them into a system as they finish each work sample. If their scores are more than two points apart, a third evaluator reads the sample. The three scores can be averaged, or the two closest scores are used. This method means that someone needs to be checking scores as they come in and making sure that work samples that need a third score are attended to.

5. At the end of each day, the scores are logged into a database for compilation and analysis.

6. The administration, assessment staff, or faculty assessment committee writes a final report that includes an analysis of the data and the findings based on that data. This report is distributed to the teaching faculty, who are then asked to write a response to the findings reporting any changes to the curriculum if needed. These reports become part of the annual assessment report. The curricular changes provide new opportunities for assessment activities and for the scholarship of teaching and learning projects. This part of the assessment process is called *closing the loop* or showing how the assessment data are used for program improvement.

7. Many programs also use the data to plan faculty development for the following year and to revise the assessment methods to ask new questions, given the findings, about how the program is doing.

Exhibit 10.4
University Studies Rubric for Critical Thinking

Score of 6—Consistently does all or almost all of the following:

- Accurately interprets evidence, statements, graphics, questions, etc.
- Identifies the salient arguments (reasons and claims) pro and con.
- Thoughtfully analyzes and evaluates major alternative points of view.
- Generates alternative explanations of phenomena or event.
- Justifies key results and procedures, explains assumptions and reasons.
- Fair-mindedly follows where evidence and reasons lead
- Makes ethical judgments

Score of 5—Does most of the following:

- Accurately interprets evidence, statements, graphics, questions, etc.
- [Thinks through issues by] Identifying relevant arguments (reasons and claims) pro and con.
- Offers analysis and evaluation of obvious alternative points of view
- Generates alternative explanations of phenomena or event.
- Justifies (by using) some results or procedures, explains reasons.
- Fair-mindedly follows where evidence and reasons leads

Score of 4—Does most of the following:

- Describes events, people, and places with some supporting details from the source.
- Makes connections to sources, either personal or analytic.
- Demonstrates a basic ability to analyze, interpret, and formulate inferences.
- States or briefly includes more than one perspective in discussing literature, experiences, and points of view of others.
- Takes some risks by occasionally questioning sources, or stating interpretations and predictions.
- Demonstrates little evidence of rethinking or refinement of ones own perspective

Score of 3—Does most or many of the following:

- Responds by retelling or graphically showing events or facts.
- Makes personal connections or identifies connections within or between sources in a limited way. Is beginning to use appropriate evidence to back ideas.

- Discusses literature, experiences, and points of view of others in terms of own experience
- Responds to sources at factual or literal level.
- Includes little or no evidence of refinement of initial response or shift in dualistic thinking.
- Demonstrates difficulty with organization and thinking is uneven

Score of 2—Does most or many of the following:

- Misinterprets evidence, statements, graphics, questions, etc.
- Fails to identify strong, relevant counter-arguments
- Draws unwarranted or fallacious conclusions
- Justifies few results or procedures, seldom explains reasons
- Regardless of the evidence or reasons, maintains or defends views based on self-interest and/or preconceptions

Score of 1—Consistently does all or almost all of the following:

- Offers biased interpretations of evidence, statements, graphics, questions, information or the points of view of others
- Fails to identify or hastily dismisses strong, relevant counter-arguments
- Ignores or superficially evaluates obvious alternative points of view. Argues using fallacious or irrelevant reasons, and unwarranted claims.
- Does not justify results or procedures, nor explains reasons.
- Exhibits close-mindedness or hostility to reason

Note. From "University Studies Rubric for Critical Thinking," by University Studies, n.d., http://www.pdx.edu/sites/www.pdx.edu.unst/files/unst_rubric_critical_thinking.pdf. Copyright 2014 by University Studies, Portland State University. Adapted with permission.

The ePortfolio assessment process is a wonderful faculty development activity. Faculty can see the level of work possible in similar classes and identify assignments that work particularly well for specific learning outcomes. They can also see what does not seem to work and find ideas to try in their own classes. It can be a very inspiring and fun time to build faculty community and discuss what student expectations should be and to develop a common understanding of the program's mission.

CONCLUSION

We do not believe that assessment is going away, and we believe that assessment can be very useful. If you are going to do the work necessary to change your practice, then knowing if those changes actually give you the results you want is critical. There are many ways to go about assessing your practices and programs. Begin with a question that is important to you, and go from there. The question can be about one class you teach or a series of classes in your department. Finding out what is really going on in your classroom is exciting and challenging but worth it.

CHAPTER 11

Parting Thoughts

Candyce's story: The master's program in educational leadership and policy that I teach requires an ePortfolio as part of our culminating project. I typically teach the course that students take to prepare for this project. This past term, one student in my class said the first day that she was anxious to get started on her ePortfolio as soon as possible. This comment was surprising, as usually students are sometimes intimidated by learning the technology required to do the project and are just nervous in general. On further exploration, it turned out that this student was a candidate for a policy position in a national organization in Washington, D.C. In her last phone interview, she was asked to send her ePortfolio if she had one. It was one of those moments that brought a smile to my face. ePortfolios were breaking through the walls of academia and entering the halls of employment. It was a sign that ePortfolios were becoming not only a promising practice in higher education but also useful in different settings.

This book introduces the concept of integrative learning and how ePortfolios can be an excellent tool for advancing it in our students. Incorporating integrative learning ePortfolios into the college curriculum is not for the faint of heart. It is not simply asking students to collect artifacts and upload them to a website. It is a complex process that takes dedication to applying the science of learning to your classroom practices to help students make the connections that they so vitally need and that allow them to integrate and deepen their learning. It is not just one assignment. It may mean changing the way you think about teaching and learning.

These changes are not without their rewards, however. Our students and students from other institutions say similar things about the impact of the process of making an ePortfolio. It has the potential to change one's relationship to oneself and expand one's understanding of personal capacities and possibilities. More than any other instructional strategy, it creates aha moments in our classrooms. How could we not become committed to integrating integrative learning ePortfolios when we have seen the impact it has had on our students' lives?

Our prediction is that ePortfolio use will continue to grow. As individual faculty and staff in colleges and universities and as institutional leaders are exposed to the practice, interest and resources will follow. Our students will ultimately forward the

149

growth of the practice. As with Candyce's student, they will need an ePortfolio as they advance beyond academe—or at least they will need to have practiced the skills in the development of an ePortfolio. As they venture into the world of work and into their communities, they will need the integrative learning skills that the Association of American Colleges and Universities (AAC&U) (2007b) has identified as an essential learning outcome of college. It is really not a matter of should we address the need, but how do we address the need. Leveraging the ePortfolio for integrative learning is a powerful way to do this.

We are stalwart proponents of ePortfolios because we think they work and we think they are fun too. We hope this book helps you see the benefits of ePortfolios, and we hope you enjoy your journey.

We would like to leave you with a few parting thoughts:

- There is no one right way to craft or teach the ePortfolio. Part of the fun is the creativity in developing integrative learning outcomes and thinking about how to teach them in the classroom. The possibilities for an ePortfolio are endless.
- The important thing is to begin. Get ePortfolios and integrative learning started in your courses, in your program, in your institution.
- Keep it small to make sure the effort is successful. Then share the results. You'll get good feedback and will likely inspire others to think about using ePortfolios.
- Remember, it gets easier every time you use ePortfolios. If you are worried about any step of the process, know that it will get better with practice. This is what we teach our students, and this lesson applies to us too.
- ePortfolios continue to expand in terms of usage and acceptance. In other words, it is worth the effort. Lead the way to the next best ePortfolio practices.
- Enjoy the ride. As you think about your own teaching and include integrative learning outcomes and ePortfolios in your practices, you will learn more about yourself as a teacher and more about your students.
- Be prepared to have your mind blown. Students will surprise you with what they create.

References

Anderson, L. W., & Krathwohl, D. R. (Eds.). (2001). *A taxonomy for learning, teaching, and assessing: A revision of Bloom's taxonomy of educational objectives.* New York, NY: Longman.

Andrade, H. G. (n.d.). *Understanding rubrics.* Retrieved from http://learnweb. harvard.edu/alps/thinking/docs/rubricar.htm

Angelo, T. A., & Cross, K. P. (1993). *Classroom assessment techniques: A handbook for college teachers.* San Francisco, CA: Jossey-Bass.

Arum, R., & Roksa, J. (2011) *Academically adrift: Limited learning on college campuses.* Chicago, IL: University of Chicago Press.

Ash, S. L., & Clayton, P. H. (2009). *Learning through critical reflection: A tutorial for service-learning students.* Raleigh, NC: Author.

Association of American Colleges and Universities. (2007a). *College learning for the new global century.* Washington, DC: Author.

Association of American Colleges and Universities. (2007b). *Liberal education and America's promise: 21st century markers for the value of US degrees and social responsibility: Integrative liberal learning for the Global Commons.* Retrieved from http://www.aacu.org/leap/index.cfm

Association of American Colleges and Universities. (n.d.). VALUE: *Valid Assessment of Learning in Undergraduate Education.* Retrieved from http://www.aacu.org/value /rubrics/index_p.cfm?CFID=13089876&CFTOKEN=61143662

Bloom, B. S. (Ed.). (1956). *Taxonomy of educational objectives: The classification of educational goals. Handbook 1: Cognitive domain.* New York, NY: David McKay.

Boag, P. (2011). *Why white space matters.* Retrieved from http://boagworld.com/ design/why-whitespace-matters/

Bolton, G. (2010). *Reflective practice: Writing and professional development.* London, UK: Sage.

Boud, D., Keogh, R., & Walker, D. (Eds.). (1985). *Reflection: Turning experience into learning.* London, UK: Routledge.

Bransford, J. D., Brown, A. L., & Cocking, R. R. (Eds.). (1999). *How people learn: Brain, mind, experience, and school.* Washington, DC: National Academies Press.

Brookfield, S. D. (1990). Using critical incidents to explore learners' assumptions. In J. Mezirow (Ed.), *Fostering critical reflection in adulthood* (pp. 177–193). San Francisco, CA: Jossey-Bass.

Cambridge, B. L. (2001). Electronic portfolios and knowledge builders. In B. L. Cambridge, S. Kahn, D. P. Perkins, & K. B. Yancey (Eds.), *Electronic portfolios: Emerging practices in student, faculty, and institutional learning* (pp. 1–11). Washington, DC: American Association for Higher Education.

Cambridge, D. (2010). *ePortfolios for lifelong learning and assessment.* San Francisco, CA: Wiley.

Cambridge, D., Chen, H. L., & Ketcheson, K. (2004). *Individual and institutional folio thinking.* Retrieved from http://www.educause.edu/library/resources/individual-and-institutional-folio-learning

Chen, H. L., & Penny Light, T. (2010). *Electronic portfolios and student success: Effectiveness, efficiency, and learning,* Washington, DC: Association of American Colleges and Universities.

Chen, H. L., Penny Light, T., & Ittleson, J. C. (2012). *Documenting learning with ePortfolio: A guide for college instructors.* San Francisco, CA: Jossey-Bass.

Chickering, A. W., & Gamson, Z. F. (1987). Seven principles for good practice in undergraduate education. *AAHE Bulletin, 39*(7), 3–7.

Clemson University. (n.d.a). *Welcome to the ePortfolio program.* Retrieved from http://www.clemson.edu/academics/programs/eportfolio

Clemson University. (n.d.b). *What is an ePortfolio?* Retrieved from http://www.clemson.edu/academics/programs/eportfolio/about

Dewey, J. (1933). *How we think.* Buffalo, NY: Prometheus.

Dewey, J. (1938). *Experience and education.* New York, NY: Collier Books.

Dewey, J. (1944). *Democracy and education.* New York, NY: Free Press.

Dunlap, L., & Sult, L. (2009). Juggling and the art of the integrative assignment. *Journal of Learning Communities Research, 3*(3), 27–45.

Dweck, C. S. (1999). *Self-theories: Their role in motivation, personality, and development.* Philadelphia, PA: Psychology Press.

Fink, L. D. (2003). *Creating significant learning experiences: An integrated approach to designing college courses.* San Francisco, CA: Jossey-Bass.

Flavell, J. H. (1979). Metacognition and cognitive monitoring: A new area of cognitive-developmental inquiry. *American Psychologist, 34*(10), 906–911.

Flower, M. (n.d.). *FRINQ ePortfolio: Assignments and resources: The implementation guide.* Retrieved from: http://frinq-commons.michael-flower.com/commons/page2/portfolio.html

Garrison, W. (2013, July). *Walking the ePortfolio talk: Begin your portfolio in 4 hours.* Workshop presented at a meeting of the Association for Authentic, Experiential and Evidence-Based Learning, Boston, MA.

Garrison, W., & Ring, G. (2013, July). *Walking the ePortfolio talk: Begin your portfolio in 4 hours.* Workshop presented at meeting of the Association for Authentic, Experiential and Evidence-Based Learning, Boston, MA.

Gibbs, G. (1988). *Learning by doing: A guide to teaching and learning.* Oxford, UK: Oxford Polytechnic Further Education Unit.

Halpern, D. F., & Hakel, M. D. (Eds.). (2000). Applying the science of learning to university teaching and beyond. *New Directions for Teaching and Learning, 89.*

Hart Research Associates. (2013). *It takes more than a major: Employer priorities for college learning and student success.* Retrieved from http://www.aacu.org/leap/documents/2013_EmployerSurvey.pdf

Huber, M. T., & Hutchings, P. (2004). *Integrative learning: Mapping the terrain.* Washington, DC: Association of American Colleges and Universities.

Jenson, J. D. (2011). Promotion self-regulation and critical reflection through writing students' use of ePortfolios. *International Journal of ePortfolio, 1*(1), 49–60.

Jones, S. (n.d.). *Using reflection for assessment.* Retrieved from http://studentlife.uiowa.edu/assets/Using-Reflection-for-Assessment.pdf

Knowles, M. (1980). *The modern practice of adult education: From pedagogy to andragogy.* Englewood Cliffs, NJ: Prentice-Hall/Cambridge.

Kuh, G. D. (2009). What student affairs professionals need to know about student engagement. *Journal of College Student Development, 50*(6), 683–786.

Kuh, G. D., Kinzie, J., Schuh, J. H., & Whitt, E. J. (2010). *Student success in college: Creating conditions that matter.* San Francisco, CA: Jossey-Bass.

Labissiere, Y., & Reynolds, C. (2004). Using electronic portfolios as a pedagogical practice to enhance student learning. *Inventio, 2*(6). Retrieved from http://www.uiowa.edu/~outcomes/documents/Labissiere.pdf

Leamnson, R. (2002). *Learning: Your first job.* Retrieved from http://www.udel.edu/CIS/106/iaydin/07F/misc/firstJob.pdf

Lorenzo, G., & Ittleson, J. C. (2005). *Demonstrating and assessing student learning with ePortfolios.* Boulder, CO: EDUCAUSE Learning Initiative.

Loughran, J. J. (1996). *Developing reflective practice: Learning about teaching and learning through modeling.* Washington, DC: Palmer Press.

McLuhan, M. (1964). *Understanding media: The extensions of man.* New York, NY: McGraw-Hill.

Mezirow, J. (1990). How critical reflection triggers transformative learning. In J. Mezirow (Ed.), *Fostering critical reflection in adulthood* (pp. 1–20). San Francisco, CA: Jossey-Bass.

Mezirow, J. (1991). *Transformative dimensions of adult learning.* San Francisco, CA: Jossey-Bass.

Mezirow, J. (1997). Transformative learning: Theory to practice. *New Directions for Adult and Continuing Education, 1997*(74), 5–12.

MPortfolio. (n.d.). Retrieved from http://mportfolio.umich.edu/showcase.html

Peet, M., Lonn, S., Gurin, P., Boyer, K. P., Matney, M., Marra, T., . . . Daley, A. (2011). Fostering integrative knowledge through ePortfolios. *International journal of ePortfolios, 1*(1), 11–31.

Portfolio to Professoriate. (n.d.). Retrieved from https://sites.google.com/site/reflectiveengineeringpractice/

Reeve, J., Jang, H., Carrell, D., Jeon, S., & Barch, J. (2004). Enhancing students' engagement by increasing teachers' autonomy support. *Motivation & Emotion, 28*(2), 147–169.

Reeve, J., Nix, G., & Hamm, D. (2003). The experience of self-determination in intrinsic motivation and the conundrum of choice. *Journal of Educational Psychology, 95*(2), 375–392.

Reflection. (n.d.). In *Merriam-Webster's online dictionary* (11th ed.). Retrieved from http://www.merriam-webster.com/dictionary/reflection

Rhodes, T. L. (Ed.). (2010). *Assessing outcomes and improving achievement: Tips and tools for using rubrics.* Washington, DC: Association of American Colleges and Universities.

Rogers, C. (2002). Defining reflection: Another look at John Dewey and reflective thinking. *Teachers College Record, 104*(4), 842–866.

Rogers, R. (2001). Reflection in higher education: A concept analysis. *Innovative Higher Education, 26*(1), 37–57.

Ryan, R. M., & Deci, E. L. (2000). Self-determination theory and the facilitation of intrinsic motivation, social development, and well-being. *American Psychologist, 55*(1), 68–78.

Scheid, K. (1993). *Helping students become strategic learners: Guidelines for teaching.* Cambridge, MA: Brookline.

Schneider, C. G. (2003). *Practicing liberal education: Formative themes in the re-invention of liberal education.* Washington, DC: Association of American Colleges and Universities.

Schneider, C. G. (2009). The proof is in the portfolio. *Liberal Education, 95*(1), 1–2.

Schön, D. A. (1983). *The reflective practitioner: How professionals think in action.* New York, NY: Basic.

Stefani, L., Mason, R., & Pegler, C. (2007). *The educational potential of e-portfolios: Supporting personal development and reflective learning.* London, UK: Routledge.

Sternberg, R. (1986). Inside intelligence. *American Scientist, 74*, 137–143.

Stevens, D. D., & Levi, A. J. (2005). *Introduction to rubrics: An assessment tool to save grading time, convey effective feedback, and promote student learning.* Sterling, VA: Stylus.

Tagg, J. (2000). *Thinking about being a student: Who are you, the student?* Retrieved from http://daphne.palomar.edu/jtagg/thinking.htm

Tagg, J. (2004). Why learn? What we may be teaching our students. *About Campus,* *9*(1), 2–10.

Taylor, E. W. (2007). An update of transformative learning theory: A critical review of the empirical research (1999–2005). *International Journal of Lifelong Education,* *26*(2), 173–191.

Taylor, S. H. (2011). Engendering habits of mind and heart through integrative learning. *About Campus, 16*(5), 13–20.

Thoman, E., & Jolls, T. (2004). Media literacy: A national priority for a changing world. *American Behavioral Scientist, 48*(1), 18–29.

Vandervelde, J. M. (2012). *EPortfolio (digital portfolio) rubric.* Retrieved from https://www2.uwstout.edu/content/profdev/rubrics/eportfoliorubric.html

Virginia Tech. (2014). *Eportfolio initiatives at Virginia Tech: Electronic portfolios.* Retrieved from https://eportfolio.vt.edu/aboutUs/index.html

Walvoord, B. E. (n.d.). *Rubric to score writing.* Retrieved from https://www.azwestern.edu/learning_services/instruction/center_teaching_effect/resources/downloads/Writing%20Rubric%20Barbara%20Walvoord.pdf

Wiggins, G., & McTighe, J. (2005). *Understanding by design.* New York, NY: Pearson.

University Studies. (n.d.). *2011–12 ePortfolio assignment: Student handout.* Retrieved from https://sites.google.com/a/pdx.edu/eportresources/frinq-eportfolio-assignment

Zull, J. E. (2002). *The art of changing the brain: Enriching the practice of teaching by exploring the biology of learning.* Sterling, VA: Stylus.

Index

with other faculty in constructing common rubrics, and how to use rubrics that someone else has constructed. The book focuses on rubrics but offers a great deal of advice about good teaching, good collaboration, and good assessment. In short, this book is a great tool."

—Barbara E. Walvoord

22883 Quicksilver Drive
Sterling, VA 20166-2102

Subscribe to our e-mail alerts: www.Styluspub.com

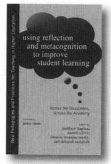

Using Reflection and Metacognition to Improve Student Learning
Across the Disciplines, Across the Academy
Edited by Matthew Kaplan, Naomi Silver, Danielle LaVaque-Manty, and Deborah Meizlish
Foreword by James Rhem

Research has identified the importance of helping students develop the ability to monitor their own comprehension and to make their thinking processes explicit, and indeed demonstrates that metacognitive teaching strategies greatly improve student engagement with course material.

This book—by presenting principles that teachers in higher education can put into practice in their own classrooms—explains how to lay the ground for this engagement, and help students become self-regulated learners actively employing metacognitive and reflective strategies in their education.

Electronic Portfolios 2.0

Emergent Research on Implementation and Impact
Edited by Darren Cambridge, Barbara Cambridge, and Kathleen Blake Yancey

"The book contains a wealth of data from schools that have been pioneers in the use of electronic portfolios. The authors identify emerging new critical questions, challenges, and opportunities for further development of this genre. A school seeking to integrate this pedagogiecal strategy will find this to be a helpful reference volume."

—*Teaching Theology and Religion*

This book features emergent results of studies from 20 institutions that have examined effects on student reflection, integrative learning, establishing identity, organizational learning, and designs for learning supported by technology. It also describes how institutions have responded to multiple challenges in ePortfolio development, from engaging faculty to going to scale.

Introduction to Rubrics
An Assessment Tool to Save Grading Time, Convey Effective Feedback, and Promote Student Learning
Dannelle D. Stevens and Antonia J. Levi
Foreword by Barbara E. Walvoord

SECOND EDITION

"A rubric, the authors emphasize, is a tool. And their book itself is a wonderful tool for exploring how to use rubrics as tools. For a long time, I have been recommending the first edition to faculty in workshops I lead. I can recommend this second edition with even greater enthusiasm, because it does so much more, and does it so intelligently.

The authors offer advice about all the surrounding situations and problems that may accompany rubrics: how to get students involved in rubrics, how to use rubrics with TAs, how to collaborate